TABLE FOR FIVE

A FATHER'S STORY OF LIFE, LOVE AND LOSS

TED YANG

"The Duke of York" is a children's nursery
rhyme, derived from a 1642 song attributed to
the stage clown Richard Tarlton.

Published by TMYC, Inc.

ISBN: 9798696530215

Cover design by: Chris Van Howten

Printed in the United States of America

DEDICATION

Table for Five is dedicated to Dr. Robert Roth—former head of the NICU in UCSF, head of premature transport in California and our personal late-night attending physician and confessor through the difficult early years. Sadly, Dr. Bob passed away in 2016.

This book is also dedicated to Dianne Legister, one of Sofia's longest-serving and most-dedicated nurses. Dianne could put a smile on all of us even during the hardest of times. She too passed away, far too early, and the world still feels that loss.

ACKNOWLEDGEMENTS

This book would not have been possible without the support of my family, especially my wife Christine and my children Sofia and Daniel.

Thanks to the alpha and beta readers and all the friends who helped this first-time author get his story on to the page and to refine it from there.

Thanks to Chris Van Howten for the fantastic cover design.

Special thanks to super editor Vira Mamchur Schwartz, without which this mess would never have become something people will want to read (I hope!)

And thanks to you for reading my story. If you've enjoyed it, I would really appreciate it if you would share it with a friend.

TABLE OF CONTENTS

Becoming a father is one of the great joys of life. The arrival of a new baby is normally a glorious celebration for the family, but the reality is that not all births go as planned. Complications leading to premature birth can occur at any time—and especially in the birth of triplets.

Mums alone bear the brunt of the pain and trauma of childbirth, but dads can feel it intensely—albeit in a less physical way. A premature birth, a baby's illness, affects both parents who long to bring a son or daughter home. Reading Ted's story, which really held my attention and learning many of these details for the first time, I am struck by the devotion that Ted has for this family. He pushed everything aside so that his world could revolve around his new family, supporting his wife, fighting for his children, and dealing with medical minutiae that most of us never go near.

I was born a month early in 1956. Modern medical science at the time was enough to keep me growing. There were no months spent in hospital with scared parents by my crib. I was one of the lucky ones.

The Yang Triplets, born at 24 weeks, started on a different and difficult path. Ted and Christine were denied the precious moments of holding newborn sons and daughter in their arms as they made their first cry. As parents, they first had to fight to make sure their children were living and breathing.

But when the worst happens and they lose a child, where does a parent find the strength to go on? Where does a parent find the strength to watch machines breathing for their daughter day in and day out? Ted gives an incredibly moving account of endless day and night trips to hospital and how even untrained but loving parents can become lifesavers and advocates for their son and daughter. And, somehow, Ted keeps his sense of humor and never loses faith that they will pull through in the end.

We all want and assume our children will arrive as perfect little people, but chance and fate throw up the most extraordinary challenges. Overcoming these challenges, no matter how awful or difficult, changes our perspective on the world and changes us for the better.

For mothers, fathers, and children, this book is an extraordinary account of joy turning into sorrow and back again. In this year of COVID-19, *Table for Five*, a rollercoaster ride of human emotion, should be a "go to" for prospective and current parents for it reminds us of how the human spirit can overcome what seem like impossible odds where the survival of tiny babies is concerned.

George Herbert
8th Earl of Carnarvon
Highclere Castle, UK

INTRODUCTION

I recall the births of my two children as moments of pure joy filled with hope, possibility, and love. My children's births were also moments of great relief—the end of long waits filled with the usual unknowables and what-ifs that all parents experience. This was especially true of my son's birth; during my wife's pregnancy we dealt with the very possible but unrealized threat of premature birth, a threat I was all too familiar with as a pediatrician and intensive care specialist.

For my wife and me, our children's births were moments that allowed us to embrace the intense bonding that comes from holding your newborn child, introducing him or her to your loved ones, and taking on the role of parent. I am deeply grateful for those experiences and for having two healthy children, now healthy adults. I also know how fortunate my family has been.

One baby out of ten is born prematurely. As a doctor, I know that for many of those families, their baby's birth is the start of a new ordeal—one that blends the hope of parenthood with the fear of new unknowns and the kinds of decisions that no parent should ever have to contemplate. For some families, birth is followed all too soon with the pain of loss: As many as one million babies die each year around the world because they are born prematurely.

As a clinician, I know well how to understand, diagnose, and treat the health problems of childhood, including those related to being born prematurely. I can effectively share the probabilities of having one problem or another as well as one outcome or another. As a healthcare executive, I understand what it takes to develop and support a team to drive the best possible outcomes. Through my experience, I can tell a family what they are likely to see and hear. I can tell them the range of problems, treatments, and outcomes that have been experienced by children like theirs. I can also help frame the difficult decisions that some families will be asked to make.

What I cannot do with any real credibility is help people understand or anticipate the experience of having a baby born prematurely, of having a child whose life is threatened by illness, or of bearing the pain of losing a child. Yet, I can appreciate how valuable and helpful it is for both parents and caregivers to see those journeys through the eyes of a parent.

While every parent experiences parenthood differently, whether their children are healthy or facing the most challenging of health problems, there are elements of each personal account that generate great insight. Ted and Christine Yang began their family with a journey that no parent would wish for, amplified by the experience of caring for triplets born far too early. Ted's account of his and his family's experience is unique, honest, and insightful.

Childhood illness is certainly a family experience, but, for many reasons, mothers and fathers will have different experiences and different perspectives on those experiences. Still, most accounts have been shared from a mother's perspective. *Table for Five* is unique in that it reflects that experience through a father's eyes. Without wanting to suggest that perspectives are defined by gender or family role, Ted's account is important in how it reflects the complementary viewpoint as a father.

I have had the privilege of having leadership roles in two of the institutions that participated in the care of Daniel, Raymond, and Sofia Yang. I deeply value the opportunity to have gotten to know Ted and his family. As a caregiver and healthcare leader, it is a gift to be able to see through the eyes of those we have been privileged to serve. There is also something we can all learn about life's important priorities from someone that has had to confront and ultimately be shaped by the unexpected need to navigate a new path.

I have been grateful for Ted's willingness to share his experience and his insight, first through a decade of conversations over the course of our friendship and now through his writing. I know you will find his story as inspiring, moving, and perspective building as I have.

Michael Apkon, M.D., Ph.D.
Former CEO, Tufts Medical Center
CEO, Hospital for Sick Children (SickKids)
CMO, Children's Hospital of Philadelphia
VP, Yale New Haven Children's Hospital

PROLOGUE

LUNCHES WITH STRANGERS

How many kids do you have? Easy question, right? That's why it is a staple of small talk. But it will never be easy for my wife or me to answer it.

I'm a serial entrepreneur, which means, among other things, that I eat lunches with strangers for a living. So I have to answer this question again and again and again.

I have three children. I *had three* children.

The IRS will tell you I have two. There are times when I say that I have two and try to leave it at that. But that leaves the typical follow-up question: "How old are your children?"

When I answer that I have two 12-year-olds, usually the immediate reply I get is automatic, redundant, and meaningless: "Oh, twins." In my case, however, it isn't meaningless at all because my wife gave birth to triplets at 24 weeks.

Now what answer do I give? Do I say "yes," and with those three letters blot out the brief but important life of my son Raymond? Or do I go deeper, explain the two are triplets and shift the entire tone of the conversation, spending the next 20 minutes going through all of the struggles that we've faced and still face today?

Is it too much information? Too personal?

I don't believe it is. I choose to reveal my story because it defines me and inspires how I approach life and business. And for all the awkward silences, sincere and heartfelt words, and fumbled apologies I'm met with after putting myself through yet another retelling of my story, every now and then, I find myself surprised. For every now and then, I hear, "You know, we lost a child, too" or "Our child was born at 26 weeks…"

When I hear that, I know I'm not alone. My story—our stories—needs telling, and not just as a catharsis for me, but as a way to give others the chance to tell their stories in return. There is something in the telling, the sharing, that brings understanding, even if it is only to know that we are not alone.

So when today's new lunch friend inevitably asks: "How many kids do you have?"

My answer is: "Let me tell my story."

CHAPTER 1

WHY MY WIFE HATES FLEETWOOD MAC

"Everything is going as great as possible..."
— *Yang Triplets Blog, September 4, 2008*

A premature baby is defined as an infant born before 37 weeks gestation. With triplets, we knew that number would be lower, closer to 32 weeks. We never expected it to be as low as 24 weeks.

I remember the drive that day. Vividly. My palms were sweaty. The steering wheel was slick in my hands, but the car was responsive. I hurtled down I-95 with the speedometer pinned to the right. I weaved between the cars and trucks, fully in the zone. I had no idea how fast I was going, I only knew I had to go faster.

Luckily, traffic was light on 95 and there were no police cars around—unusual for Connecticut at any time and no less so that September 4, 2008—and I made it back to Yale-New Haven Hospital from my job in Westport in record time, well under the 35 to 40 minutes or so it would usually take.

My tires squealed as I pulled into the parking lot. I stopped moving just long enough to look up and see a rainbow. It was a small one and a little hazy. I would never call myself superstitious, but I couldn't help but hope that it was a good omen. I sprinted through the entrance, up the elevator, down the hall, and arrived, out of breath, back at the exact same room I had left just hours ago.

When my wife of five years, Christine, went into her 23rd week of pregnancy, she started having light contractions. Up to that point everything had been fine—at least as fine as it can be with triplets. For a

week she had been upstairs in the hospital going through the equivalent of extreme bed rest, which included 52 hours of being in a bed tilted at a 45-degree angle to stave off labor. She vacillated between daylong calm periods and sudden, sharp contractions. I would hold her hand and whisper encouragement to her, and we kept stretching it out one day

The actual rainbow from that day.

at a time, hoping those days would quickly add up and get us out of this very dangerous situation.

The previous night, Christine had a particularly strong contraction, which required moving her down to the perinatal ward. Upon hearing this, I left work immediately, drove up to the hospital, and joined her.

Hospitals are confusing, impersonal places at best and this ward was no different. Birthing room after birthing room was filled with moms and families. Some, like my wife, were trying to hold off birth, others were in active labor, and still others were recovering.

I settled in for a long night with Christine, set on keeping her spirits up and filling whatever role she needed me to play. They started her on various IV drips, all designed to stop her worsening contractions.

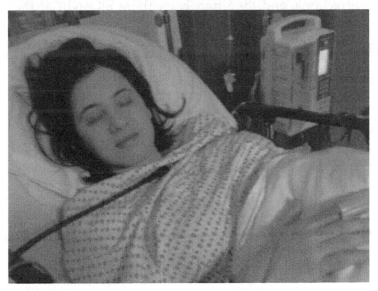

Christine in the hospital, soon to give birth.

I don't remember dozing, but I must have. When I awoke the next morning, September 4, things had stabilized. The doctors said that the drugs were taking effect and that it would be ok for me to go back to work—that nothing was likely to happen for 24 to 48 hours.

Of course they were wrong. Not half an hour after I surprised my co-workers by arriving at a meeting in Westport, I got the call no father-to-be wants to receive. Our daughter's placenta was separating and my wife was starting to exhibit signs of preeclampsia, a life-threatening condition for a pregnant woman. My daughter and her two brothers needed to be delivered immediately.

My in-laws were in Christine's room when I arrived back at the hospital. They had come to stay with us when things got dicey the week before when Christine started exhibiting discomfort and light contractions, and they had been there all night at the hospital as well. These were their first grandchildren, although they hadn't been expected to be the first. My wife's sister was pregnant as well and her child should have been born before ours.

The four of us barely fit in the room; with my wife in her bed, the quarters were close and dark. And now that Christine was being prepped for surgery, the room suddenly seemed blindingly bright and noisy. Or maybe that was just the ringing in my head. I would be a father—not once, but three times over—before the day was done.

CRCRCRCRCR

Like most couples, Christine and I had struggled to find names we agreed on. After what seemed like days of back and forth, we found Sofia, a name we both loved, for our daughter. We knew we didn't want our kids to have the same names as everybody else, and going with my wife's Italian side, we chose the more unique spelling for her name (as opposed to Sophia).

It took a little longer for us to decide on the boys' names. When we found we both really liked Daniel it was a relief. Agreeing on Raymond was even easier. I had lost an Uncle Raymond to cancer and my wife had lost an Uncle Raymond as well.

We didn't believe in bad luck, but maybe we should have.

I also wanted our children to have Chinese names. Even though I was teased incessantly in school for my middle name, I wanted to follow this tradition in naming our children. Heritage is important to Christine and me, and despite my various struggles fitting in as a child, I wanted their middle names to celebrate their Chinese ancestry.

My Chinese name, Ming-Teh, is my middle name. It follows the traditional pattern of being composed of two parts: The first part is a generational name meant to be shared across every child and the second is my personal name. Ming means bright or smart and Teh means moral or ethical. (Definitely wishful thinking by my parents!)

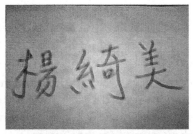

Sofia Chi-Mei Yang

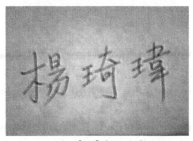

Raymond Chi-Wei Yang

So I wrote the names on the hospital room's whiteboard, carefully copying my mother's handwriting for the Chinese names: The three Yang babies were to be Sofia Chi-Mei, Raymond Chi-Wei, and Daniel Chi-Long, with Chi as their

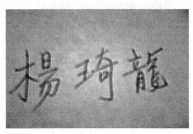

Daniel Chi-Long Yang

generational name. Chi means extremely or very much and Mei, Wei and Long mean pretty, great/kingly, and dragon respectively.

My mother-in-law Polley, upon hearing the names for the first time in Christine's hospital room, started to tear up. We all knew that one third of babies born at 24 weeks didn't make it, one third ended up just fine, and one-third went through hell. I can't recall what we said to each other in that moment, but we knew things were about to change, drastically—even in the best-case scenario. And the best case was very, very unlikely.

A nurse came in to ask if I wanted to be at the birth. Of course I did. I started to feel the tingle of nerves as I came down off my adrenaline high that had got me to Yale in record time and ran to the bathroom. I had just enough time to wash up and put on a gown before they came to usher me into the operating room.

C8C8C8C8C8

For the longest time I didn't want kids. This was partly because I knew my life was busy and hectic—I had a lot I wanted to do—but it was also because my own family wasn't close. And while I never had a close relationship with my father growing up, I inherited his temper, and I worried about what kind of father that would make me.

It's amazing what a loving partner and the drumbeat of biology will do, though. By the time we started talking about getting married I had come around to wanting children. Christine had always hoped to be a mother.

We know the exact day our children were conceived. I know it may seem a little unbelievable, but we were timing for maximum effect. The right day turned out to be the same exact day that we were moving into our new house in New Canaan, Connecticut.

You can picture the scene: moving truck unloading box after box, my wife and I furiously searching for enough of our linens to put on the just-reassembled bed. We were tired, but duty called! Then we settled in for an evening of unpacking and Domino's Pizza. Little did we know just how well maximized our timing turned out to be.

Two weeks later, on April 11, 2008, the boxes were gone and the doctor confirmed it: Christine was pregnant.

A month later it was clearer still: Christine was pregnant with twins.

A month after that the bottom fell out: Christine was pregnant with triplets.

One of the questions we usually get asked is whether or not we had IVF. Nope, but we did have a little help. We started trying to get pregnant in August 2007, and after several months without result, we turned to our doctors. Christine was diagnosed with Polycystic Ovarian Syndrome, which is a fancy way of saying that she didn't ovulate regularly. The doctor prescribed Clomid, a drug that acts to release eggs, at the lowest possible dosage

It was on my wife's first cycle with Clomid that a blood test confirmed the pregnancy and the elevated hormone levels presaging twins. Her doctor at the time was quite surprised by the drug's effectiveness, but we have since found out that it isn't that uncommon. Additionally, twins run in my wife's family and so we were both actually hoping for them. I liked the idea of the kids having an instant best friend. And wouldn't it be cool if they turned out to be identical? So when we went into her first ultrasound to confirm the number of heartbeats, we were already excited.

They found one, then two, and, then, of course, three heartbeats. The room was cold to begin with but I distinctly remember shivering. Christine recalls the excitement of three suddenly shifting to fear as the doctor rattled off all the complications and things that could go wrong. My wife took my hand for support. The doctor wasn't particularly happy to see three embryos, given the risks, and neither were we.

We knew that we wanted three kids, but… could we handle this?

Yes, we'd gotten most of the traveling in that we wanted to before we would become parents. We did all the going out and the hanging out we thought we needed to do. We had the house, steady income, insurance. Our parents lived near-by. We were as prepared as we could be to have a family. Now we had to decide if we were ready to have it all at once.

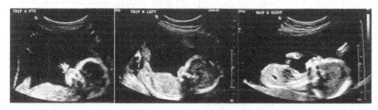

Baby A (Sofia), Baby B (Raymond), and Baby C (Daniel).

In that moment, though, there wasn't any decision to be made. One of the three embryos, "A," was significantly smaller than the other two, and we were told that it would likely "self-terminate" and dissolve into its siblings while dissolving the risks associated with having triplets. So week after week, we repeated the ultrasound, looking to see what would happen. A wasn't giving up. On the contrary, A was catching up, growing and growing. Chorionic villus sampling (CVS—a prenatal test that can determine birth defects and other problems during pregnancy) at 10 to 11 weeks revealed that all three were genetically healthy and viable.

Now came the decision. We had been told and learned from other families that the odds were significantly more favorable for twins than triplets. According to the March of Dimes, 90 percent of all triplets (and higher multiples) are born premature. In fact, while 85 percent of triplets survive, almost 98 percent of twins do. Furthermore, there was a far higher risk of prematurity, with triplets birthing at 32 weeks' gestation on average. This is why many doctors counsel "reducing" triplets to twins in what is essentially a selective abortion.

We didn't really understand prematurity at the time, so we went to visit Neo-Natal Intensive Care Units (NICUs) in the area, including the one in Yale-New Haven Hospital. The attending doctor (the senior-most neonatologist in charge each day) on duty toured us around the ward. She reiterated the stats we were told before, but also stressed that each decision was individual. We saw other parents going through a struggle that we knew could be ours soon and came to the conclusion that we wanted to give our kids the best chance possible and reduce the pregnancy.

Except, as the weeks passed and we saw A grow larger and larger, we became less and less sure of our path. As the time of decision approached (Christine was at 13 weeks), we were no closer to finding a resolution. We still went to Columbia Presbyterian Hospital in New York City for our appointment with the specialist that would consult on the procedure, but we felt uncertain. The traffic on the way there was heavy and slow; there was a lack of close parking when we arrived. Everything contributed to the general sense that we didn't belong there.

Throughout the consult, what kept going through my mind was that there was a missing piece of information:

whether or not the reduction process itself introduced risk. We were assured that it did not, but it was obvious to me that the doctors were glossing over the details.

Evaluating risk was part of what I did back then (and still do to an extent) in my professional capacity working for a hedge fund. Numbers I get, but no one could give me the numbers I wanted to hear that would make a decision easy. Post-reduced twins logically had less of a chance than natural twins. How much, though?

Ultimately, here's what clinched it for me: A 98 percent chance of survival didn't apply to the baby that was reduced. In other words, you were 100 percent guaranteed to lose a child in exchange for increasing the odds for the other two. Was that a decision we were prepared to make... and at some point tell our surviving children about?

My wife went through a different process that was more emotional than mine, but we arrived at the same decision together: Thanks, doc, but we'll take our chances with all three.

It was obvious that the doctor felt we had made the wrong decision when Christine told her. And to the doctor, maybe it was the wrong decision. But even given the hell that we've been through, I don't for a second doubt that we made the right choice in not giving up on A, who turned out to be Sofia.

Our difficult decision made, Christine and I went on a two-week cruise to Scandinavia and St. Petersburg, Russia. It was a spectacular trip, not only for the experience itself, but in that we made a very good friend of one of our co-travelers: Dr. Bob Roth, a former NICU director and hospital bigwig in California. He would be invaluable to us in the times ahead, and this book is dedicated to him.

CSCSCSCSCS

The operating room met all of the expectations I'd formed watching television and movies. Blindingly bright lights? Check. Lots of people in gowns (including myself)? Check. Lots of machines making lots of beeps? Check. The smell of antiseptic, which I would become all too familiar with? Check.

By the time I was hustled in through the double doors, my wife was already on the table, trying not to squirm as a spinal block was administered. I couldn't see her face. They had set up a privacy screen so that all I saw was her bottom half as they prepped for surgery.

I walked over to the other side of the screen and there she was, smiling at me. I know I'm supposed to say that I had never seen her look so beautiful or her eyes so bright, but honestly, I wasn't thinking about that. I was scared for her and our children. In her eyes I saw bravery. Christine knew what was about to happen—or at least what could happen—and there she was, gathering all her strength to do it anyway.

I took her hand and smiled at her. I'm sure I cracked a joke, but I can't remember any specifics. It couldn't have been very funny because the nurse that was dedicated to taking care of her didn't smile.

On the other side of the screen, the doctors and nurses were busy doing their thing, so my wife and I were only responsible for making one decision just then. Behind Christine, there was a good old-fashioned CD player. No iPod with its thousands of songs in hundreds of genres here. They actually had three or four classic rock CDs to pick from that were probably the favorites of the operating room staff.

Not seeing any Led Zeppelin—in that moment, Christine couldn't have cared less about music choices—I reached for Fleetwood Mac's *Greatest Hits* and put it on random. And so, the soundtrack to our great adventure was set. Then the world slowed down.

Track 1
Track 2
Track 3

And finally, sometime around "Rhiannon," things started to happen. They had brought a stool for me to sit on, but I couldn't sit down. I was standing and looking over the screen when they made the incision to begin the caesarean section. Some sort of self-preservation instinct must have kicked in because I can't remember any of the gory details. It didn't take long at all before out came Baby A, Sofia, blue, bloody, and precious. My wife, thanks to the curtain and the drugs, didn't notice anything and asked me what was going on. She was surprised to hear that she had started to give birth.

Do premature babies cry when they come out? Mine did not. At least, I have no memory of them crying, Christine, however, remembers hearing Sofia cry. We barely saw Sofia before she was whisked away into a separate operating theatre.

Track 5

And then baby boys B and C, who were further in the womb than their more eager sister, came out simultaneously. Welcome to the world: Raymond and Daniel! Once again, we got a quick peek before they were whisked away. I can't imagine that what we saw was different from any parent seeing their children born by c-section. None of the hell that we were about to go through had happened yet, and while we were braced for it, none of it mattered. All that mattered was seeing these brave, beautiful new lives. I kissed my wife and told her I loved her.

Now that the delivery was over, her nurse assured Christine that she was doing great and that they

Sofia Chi-Mei Yang - 660gm 11:54 a.m.
Raymond Chi-Wei Yang - 640gm 11:57 a.m.
Daniel Chi-Long Yang - 680gm 11:57:02 a.m.

would have her sewn up in just a few minutes. I took the opportunity to get up, squeezed my wife's hand, and let them usher me from the room into the hall so that I could see what was going on with my children through the windows.

Which is, of course, why my wife hates Fleetwood Mac. She listened to the rest of the CD and then heard the whole thing again on repeat as they put her back together over the next hour. So much for a few minutes. One of the nurses told Christine later that they had to "put her uterus back in."

CHAPTER 2

LOSING RAYMOND

"24-Hour Mark: I'm glad to say
all three are doing fantastically."
— Yang Triplets Blog, September 5, 2008

Immediately after the children were born, they were whisked away, each attended to by their own team of doctors and nurses. All three of their tiny little bodies, barely a pound and a half each, needed a little help to survive.

Actually, it was very surprising to me exactly how little help that was initially. By the time I saw them next, each was in their own incubator and on a ventilator—and from that moment I began my training period as an unofficial respiratory therapist. Sofia, Daniel, and Raymond each had oxygen delivered at a certain pressure and rate into their lungs. I watched in sheer amazement as their tiny little chests went up and down as the machines breathed for them.

Christine was still upstairs recovering and in quite a bit of pain, so for much of that first day, she saw her children only through the pictures I had taken on my phone. Then, finally, she was brought in a wheelchair and physically looked upon her children for the first time.

We couldn't hold them, due to the risk of infection and their tiny size, but we were still happy that things were going well. Or perhaps I should say we were cautiously happy, as we were both bracing ourselves for the end of the 24-to-48-hour preemie "honeymoon period."

It really did seem like things were getting better. Sofia was the first to come off her ventilator. Then Daniel started breathing on his own a few minutes at a time. Our children, who were born four months too early, were starting to breathe on their own? We'd been expecting tragedy and here were these major (if tentative) victories. Or were these early successes only setting us up for a bigger fall?

Personally, I've always taken pride in being pretty even-keeled when I need to be, even though I'm a very passionate person (and have the aforementioned temper). When things go well I don't let myself get too happy, and when things start to go poorly, I don't let myself get too upset. But this particular strength of mine was about to be tested.

Two days in, Raymond started to lag behind. While his sister was off the vent and his brother was getting closer and closer to coming off, Raymond's tube got mispositioned and he stubbornly refused to acclimate to reduced breathing support. Even so, things were going well enough that by the time day four rolled around, we were feeling hopeful—even more so when we learned Christine could come home.

Some women are up and about the next day with manageable discomfort after a caesarian. Christine was not one of those women. She had endured incredible pain thanks to doctors who stubbornly refused to give her the pain medication she desperately needed and instead only gave her a baseline amount. It was only after I had some extremely choice words with the team that enough morphine was finally administered. The pain from major surgery lingered and it took her a few extra days to recover.

So Christine was home. I was home. Mentally, emotionally, however, we remained at that hospital.

We would come home to sleep, change clothes, and go back. We'd sit and stand by the incubators, watching, talking to Sofia, Daniel, and Raymond, urging them on from the sidelines as if we were at a

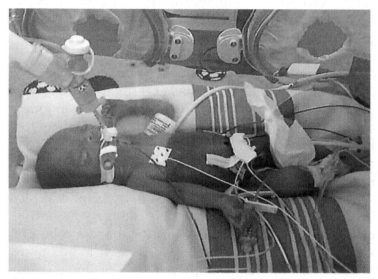

Raymond hooked up to his tubes and monitors.

hoped-for future soccer game. I asked questions of staff, nodded hello to fellow NICU parents when we happened to make eye contact, and hoped and waited. I can't recall what Christine and I talked about. For four days this was our routine.

There was no such thing as paternity leave at that time at Bridgewater (or anywhere in America!) and my job was very demanding so Christine and I knew I would have to go back sooner or later in some capacity. I decided on sooner. In retrospect this seems absurd. With three kids in the NICU five days after their birth and my wife newly at home, exactly what was so important at work? It turned out it wasn't my boss who needed me and it wasn't my team. It was *me* needing to put my energies into thinking about something else, anything else than ventilators and babies. Me needing to be in a situation I knew how to fix and control. How naïve that all seems now.

When I was younger, I would get upset at everything that went wrong. I tried to control everything precisely to keep them from going wrong. People who know me and read this will probably say that I haven't changed, but I've calmed down about it a lot. Life teaches you, teaches all of us, that there are things we can fix and control and others we simply can't. And it's a hard lesson to learn.

Somehow I was still able to work while things continued to deteriorate for Raymond. His red and white blood cell counts dropped precipitously, indicating a bleed or an infection. Scans indicated that it wasn't the former, so, anticipating the latter, they started him on a heavy-duty antibiotic and upped his breathing support to an oscillating ventilator right as I was coming into the NICU on September 9th.

You've probably seen a regular ventilator on a TV show. It looks like a grey or beige box with lots of dials and LED gauges. Connected to the box are two plastic pipes. These are the most important part of the ventilator as they connect to the breathing tube, which goes inside your child. The vent makes a whoosh-whoosh sound that emulates breathing, pushing oxygenated air in and taking carbon dioxide out many times a minute.

An oscillating vent is more like a prop out of a science-fiction movie. Instead of a bland-colored box, there is a shiny metal ellipsoid—kind of like a flat football that is mounted on a cube. The cube does lead to the same two tubes that go into the child, but instead of a reassuring whoosh-whoosh, it makes a fast-pitched whirring sound hundreds of times a minute as it cycles air through. It looks and sounds slightly menacing, like high-tech alien machinery.

I took one glance at this... thing connected to Raymond and my heart sank. For the first time, it started to hit home that it might *not* go well for Raymond. Christine and I, however, were not ready to speak aloud our fears.

Have you ever gotten a sudden idea while driving to pull the steering wheel hard to the right, even though that would surely drive you off the road? You would never do it, but still, for a millisecond the idea is there in your brain. Studies show about half the population has experienced this sensation. It's an intrusive, sudden thought. The term for it is the "call of the void," and that is exactly what I felt when I saw the alien cube. I wanted to pull that tube out. Part of me was 100 percent certain he was already dead and wanted to rip the contraption to shreds.

I didn't, of course, but that night when we left our three in the hospital, I think I was already saying goodbye to a child I had barely met.

On the morning of the sixth day after their birth, doctors confirmed that Raymond had an infection, specifically gram negative rods (E. Coli is part of this group). It didn't take much googling to find out that this type of infection was the leading cause of NEC, the dreaded necrotizing enterocolitis that is the bane of preemie babies. It attacks and destroys their underdeveloped intestines and digestive system, triggering a cascade of ancillary problems that often results in death. Nevertheless, we continued to hold out hope as the identification of a culprit meant that the doctors could target Raymond with specific and not just general antibiotics.

As it turned out, that was all they could do, other than treat the symptoms. As Raymond's system continued to break down, the most prominent symptom was swelling. It was pretty clear that something was seriously wrong with him just by looking at him, but we thought that he would come out of it; he'd gone through several ups and downs in his short existence already.

Our biggest fear was that brain damage would impair his quality of life, but the scans didn't show bleeding around the brain. Unfortunately, that still didn't guarantee that there wasn't any impairment; micro-damage to brain cells was still possible, but we remained hopeful because no bleed was still a very, very good sign—especially this many days into the infection.

The next morning I went into the office while Christine went directly to the hospital. What was so important that I had to be at work while my son was fighting for his life? Who knows? I can't even remember what I was working on let alone its importance. What I do vividly recall is the telephone call later that morning and the conversation that followed.

The call from the hospital relayed that things had drastically changed: Raymond had a grade- four (out of four) brain bleed, which meant that not only was there bleeding in his brain tissue but that it was un-contained, pervasive, and leaking into his other tissues. I went into my boss's office, the nondescript office of the chief technology officer of the world's largest hedge fund, Bridgewater Associates, and sat down across from his desk. Our conversation went something like this:

> Me: "I need to go the hospital and I won't be back for many days."
>
> Boss: "Ok, sure, whatever you need, Ted. What happened?"
>
> Me: "Raymond has a brain bleed. It's grade four which means..."
>
> Boss: (waiting)
>
> Me: "Which means..."
>
> Boss: (still waiting)
>
> Me: "He's dead."

I wouldn't give up on baby A because I wouldn't trade her life for an improved chance of life for her brothers. Would I now give up on Raymond? I felt the percentages calling me. Was I being punished for my hubris by being given a far, far more difficult choice?

The prognosis for a grade-four brain bleed caused by sepsis (NEC) in a severely premature baby is not good. Actually, it's worse than not good: It's terrible. Raymond, *if* he survived to childhood, would have severe impairment from severe brain damage; in fact, developmentally he might never reach adulthood. He had essentially a zero chance of having a typical, pain-free life.

Now we had to decide the unthinkable: Do we keep Raymond alive no matter the pain to him? Or do we let him go?

How could I, who had the means and was a believer in medicine and science, not do absolutely everything I could to keep him alive?

Or were all of the efforts we made not really for Raymond or the quality of *his* life; were they to make *us* feel like we'd tried?

Just the day before Raymond had a brain bleed, we had spoken with Dr. Bob, our new friend from the trip a few months back, as well as with the attending doctors and we all agreed to do everything we could for Raymond—that we would see where it goes, wait for more information with the hopes that the situation would turn around. News of the grade-four brain bleed changed everything.

It was the fact that Raymond would live a life of pain and struggle that got me—and Christine, too. It was this harsh future reality that led us to the devastating decision to let Raymond go by retracting his life support. We had tried everything. Medicine and science had no answer for us. How could we condemn our son to such a life?

This was *our* decision alone. Christine's and mine. We never asked either set of grandparents for their opinion in letting Raymond go. They respected our decision and no one ever tried to talk us out of it.

Christine spoke at length about the process with one of the floor nurses who explained that Raymond would be given morphine to ease his passing and we would hold him until he was gone.

Perhaps you're reading this and thinking how you would never make that decision—that you would fight until the end and love and care for that child as long as you could. All I can say is, I hope you never find yourself in such a situation. Yes, we were partly being selfish, but also we were being selfish for our other two children, who still needed us desperately.

 C8C8C8C8CB

On September 11, 2001, America suffered its worst-ever attack on our soil, a tragedy that claimed the lives of almost three thousand people. I was six blocks away when the first tower fell. My co-workers and I knew that it wouldn't be safe to stay, so we left where we had been sheltering and started walking up Hudson Street. Many other people had the same idea, and the streets were filled with them, all quickly walking—not running—uptown. Some people were crying, but mostly it was deathly quiet.

Then the screams started. I turned to look and watched as the second tower fell. Like everyone else, I stood there until we could see the cloud of dust and debris start to move towards us. Then we ran. All of us. There wasn't any logic to it; we didn't know what to do. The next thing I knew I was in the Village and still heading north in a throng. Everyone was in their own world, dealing with their own loss and their own pain. All I could think about was how I would get in touch with my wife, who was in Midtown herself, and how we could find safety in a world that was radically different than the one I left a few hours ago, when I stepped out of the World Trade Center.

Seven years later, a similar—though more intense and personal—kind of confusion, pain, and sadness was with us on September 11, 2008. I watched as they turned off and disconnected the machines and handed Raymond to me. Christine was already in the "grief room," the room that usually functioned as a lactation room but would be quickly converted as the sad need arose. Christine was used to going to that room every few hours to pump life-giving milk for her children and now she was in it to say goodbye. With the door closed, we held Raymond for the first time and last time. We each held our son in our arms as he died—

first by ourselves and then all three of us together. Right outside that door nurses were bustling about, babies were struggling to survive, and other parents were dealing with their own hopes, pain, and loss.

Christine with Raymond.

Did Daniel and Sofia sense that their brother—with whom they spent the first 24 weeks of their existence—was dying a mere 30 feet from them?

He was so small and so light. I recall his skin was soft and tight, his body puffed up with all the swelling. He didn't smell of anything except chemicals and had a few wisps of hair on his head that I ruffled lightly. It took a long time for Raymond's heart to stop beating. His tiny, perfect hands and feet were getting cold, but his heart kept going. Christine even asked the doctors to check a few times if he were truly gone.

At 6:28 p.m. on September 11, 2008, we lost Raymond.

My wife cried. I didn't. At least, I don't recall any tears. Christine distinctly remembers a tear or two from me; it was the most emotion she'd seen from me during this whole time. This is normal for me. I didn't cry at my Uncle Raymond's funeral either, who died of cancer far too young.

I saw the sunlight through the window hit my wife as she held our son and was glad he was at peace. I'm sure we said something to each other but the details remain a blur in my memory. I might have sung a song I planned to use as a lullaby. I did promise to tell his brother and sister about him and I told Raymond I would always love him. All our hopes for Raymond... would never be.

At some point a grief counselor came in and left, as did some of the doctors and nurses. Christine remembers only one doctor specifically coming by to express sympathy; she was a young mother herself. We spoke with our parents. I took the photo on the previous page. And sometime after that we kissed our son, said goodbye for the last time to Raymond, and drove home.

.

CHAPTER 3

THE DAY AFTER

*"It sounds funny to long to hear your child cry,
but it will be a welcome sound."*
—*Yang Triplets Blog, October 15, 2008*

The next day we woke up and went back to the same place where Raymond died. I found myself looking for three children but only found two.

The floor had been cleared, but the bay where Raymond's incubator stood had yet to be cleaned up—the detritus of wrappers, gauze, and urgency remained scattered in and around it. The monitors were all dark. I know that the nurses probably hadn't deliberately left things like that, but I'd like to think that someone thought to give us a little time before filling that bay with someone else's child.

It is amazing how clarifying death can be. When we committed to keeping all three of our children, we knew that there was a very high likelihood that at least one of our children would have significant issues. But we decided to play the percentages and hope it wouldn't happen to us. Once Christine gave birth, those odds worsened to a one-in-three mortality rate for children born at 24 weeks. When Raymond died, that abstract probability crystalized into hardened reality. As we would learn again and again, numbers are one thing, your own children quite another. It is hard to be dispassionate when you are talking about your own flesh and blood.

Nevertheless, for me, Raymond still existed as more of an abstraction than as a child. I had barely held him, except to let him go. I'm not ashamed to admit that I didn't mourn for him properly then. How could I when I had two survivors that very much needed me?

Yes, that was a rationalization. For us, for me, to continue functioning and make the proper decisions for our children we had, I had, to be cold and rational. Despite having been shown in no uncertain terms by a few billion bacteria that I was not special and that this was going to hurt, my loss was too new to me. Does it make sense that I felt bad that I didn't feel worse? Because that's the only way that I can describe it.

C3C3CGCGC3

The hospital did offer us various services after Raymond's death—people to speak with, groups to join. I declined. Looking back now, all the hospital social workers and all the counselors, they all seemed focused on the mother's loss. Christine saw the services as more children-centric; parents were never the focus and social workers were there more for triage, helping those who appeared to need it most.

Regardless, that was fine with me at the time. I've always handled tough times on my own. Christine spoke with her parents almost daily. I didn't turn to my family and I didn't turn to friends.

I don't have many close friends. I read once that a person can have at most five close friends—that number would be high for me. I consider a close friend someone that I can call at any time and talk about anything without feeling weird or uncomfortable. It's cliché, but mostly true in my case: My closest friends were from college.

Nonetheless, did I call them to talk about Raymond, about how I felt losing a child? No.

Working all hours and having moved to Connecticut less than a year before the kids were born was not conducive to making or having close friends nearby. We hadn't had time yet to befriend fellow neighborhood parents, expectant or otherwise.

Truthfully, being close to your neighbors always struck me as a bit weird. Most of my friends were naturally work friends, *aka* situational friends, since that's where I spent most of my time. After Raymond's death and the uncertainty that followed with Daniel's health and especially Sofia's, many of those friends fell by the wayside.

To be fair to them, what exactly did I expect? How were we supposed to continue to be friends when we lost what we had in common and I replaced it with something they couldn't be part of? My life was consumed with my children and theirs were still focused on work. Oh, I'm sure some of them would have responded positively if I could have asked for help, but I'm not one to ask for help. From anyone.

As word spread of what was happening, many people in our collective pasts reached out to see how they could help; Christine and I appreciated that. Unfortunately, though, there was little they could do and, frankly, we grew very tired of repeating the same stories, stuck in a tragedy from which we could not move past.

I guess I had anticipated some of that because prior to our children's birth I had started an online blog, yangtriplets.blogspot.com. We were having triplets: I

expected crazy, just not sad, stressed crazy to the levels
it reached. The blog let us keep some level of
relationships going even when we had no energy to do
so.

The Yang Triplets blog.

Because of the blog, a nurse introduced Christine to
another preemie mom (with a pretty smooth journey
compared to ours) who wanted to set up a blog of her
own. Until then Christine hadn't really interacted with
other parents during our days in the NICU. The two
have remained friendly to this day.

The blog was also a kind of support system. When
things were going badly, reading comments from
family and even random strangers who found our blog
was comforting. None of them could really understand
what was going on, but they all wanted the best for
Sofia and Daniel. That was enough to help power me
through the tough days.

ↃↄↃↄↃↄↃↄↃↄ

Still, it was a strange blow to be back in that same
room, a little more than 12 hours after Raymond died.

At Yale, the NICU used to have two distinct rooms
for the most critical infants. Each room had 10 bays,

which contained a bank of monitors and drawers of supplies and equipment. Pulled up to some of the bays was an incubator.

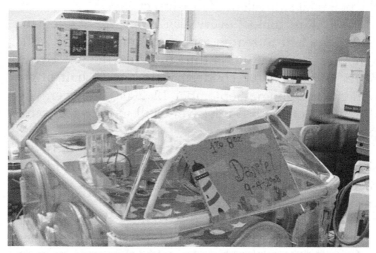

Daniel's home in the NICU.

If you haven't seen one up close, an incubator looks like a clear plastic box on wheels. The baby goes in the box, which has round cutouts so that the child can be accessed. The incubator has heat, lights, power, and all sorts of interesting doodads and alarms on it. It also has a ton of wires and hoses connecting it to oxygen, power, suction, and multiple backups.

As babies come in and out of the critical-case NICU room, their incubators are rolled up to an empty bay and hooked in. The system was designed to be super-flexible so that, when needed, extra equipment could be rolled up next to an incubator, or incubators could be moved together to make them easier to monitor by the same nurse or medical team.

You might think that they would keep the babies that were likely to be there for an extended period of time in the same spot, but when you factor in that there are three shifts each day and that most children are in that room for only a few days, what you end up with is the neonatal equivalent of musical chairs.

Therefore, almost every day when we entered the NICU, we had to search for where our children were. (This wasn't usually that difficult since the NICU was never full; our three children were almost half of the patients in a room.) September 12, 2008, however, was different: Sofia and Daniel were still in the exact same places.

Nothing had changed even though we had lost our son. That felt strange and somehow wrong. And that feeling of strangeness only got magnified as we went through morning rounds.

There were normally three shifts a day for the doctors and nurses. Since most parents experienced only a short stay, the almost weekly change in primary attending doctors wasn't an issue, but for Christine the change was frustrating. Inevitably the new attending would re-evaluate and change the plan of their predecessor. We had to learn a new way to interact with each doctor—some of whom were pessimistic in their outlooks and others more optimistic.

That also meant that a different nurse took care of our children late at night than during the day or evening. If things were calm, one nurse could cover all our children, but depending on how critical things were, we could have up to three different nurses going at the same time. To deal with it, we developed our own rituals to stay in contact with the people who were caring for our preemies.

After leaving the hospital between 7 and 8 p.m., we would call back before bed time, usually around 10 p.m., and ask to speak with the nurses who had recently come on shift for that night. That was a good time for them to update us since they had just been updated themselves. Then we would call those same nurses first thing in the morning before they left and before we ourselves headed in to the hospital sometime around 9 a.m.

If you've watched any medical television show, you know what rounds are. As a teaching hospital,

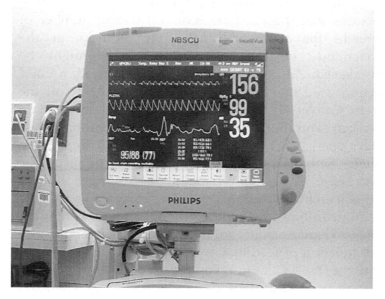

The all-important bedside monitor.

Yale had a constant supply of residents rotating through the NICU. And yes, we would see the same tired faces—in what were likely the same scrubs—time and time again. Each morning, the doctors would do rounds, spending time with each child and going through the major events of the night. They would discuss their plan for the day and talk about the parameters for making decisions as that day went by.

For example, our children were on ventilators, and as they grew stronger, their settings on the vent would be lowered in trials. In each trial, the respiratory therapist would tweak various parameters and see if the children maintained their blood oxygenation without distress. First they would bring the oxygen level down to room air (23 percent), then they would gradually reduce the amount of mechanical support the child received. This might mean that the amount of breaths that the machine took versus the number of breaths the child took might be reduced, or the magnitude of each of those breaths might be weakened. As these settings slowly lessened, a child approached the point where they might come off the vent. Conversely, if a child couldn't maintain a certain oxygen saturation (near 100 percent is ideal) or if they developed other issues that indicated distress, then their settings would stay the same or even be increased. This might happen, for example, if they caught an infection.

In addition to ventilator changes, there were other major changes that could be made: the amount and formulation of feedings, which at that early stage was sucrose by IV, administration of various drugs or vaccinations and many other treatments, for example. Then there were things to watch out for during the day like temperatures, urination, and bowel movements— you get the idea. Morning rounds set up the plan of care that was then followed the rest of that day.

Not all families participate in morning rounds. Since most of the infants are there only for a short period of time, there isn't a need. For others, morning rounds would not be productive, usually because families wouldn't be able to handle the clinical way it is conducted or the onslaught of medical lingo. And then there are those doctors who just didn't like to involve the families. While this attitude is subsiding, we still found this "old school" thinking pervading much of the medical system at that time. If I had become the doctor it was expected I would be, perhaps I would have shared that old-school attitude, but from the other side, I had no patience for it.

CRCRCRCRCR

Growing up, education was paramount. My mom loves to say that she didn't push me. That's mostly true—I was more than happy to flog myself to greater and greater academic achievement.

As far as my parents were concerned, there were only two acceptable university choices, both of which happen to be in Cambridge, Massachusetts. And there was only one acceptable career choice: medicine. In my particular case, my father came from a line of doctors, although he didn't become one himself. My great-grandfather and grandfather were doctors and two of my uncles are retired MDs. Clearly, I was expected to continue the tradition after it skipped a generation.

For the record, I would have made a terrible doctor. I knew that instinctively, which is why I didn't want to become one.

At the Massachusetts Institute of Technology, commonly MIT—the Cambridge school I settled on—plenty of my friends (including my freshman-year roommate) became doctors, so I had a lot of exposure to pre-med. I watched them take many, many "ology" classes and agonize over the MCATs to earn the privilege of taking still more classes and enduring more agony over their boards. Perhaps this is why my impression of medicine was always that it was a science—that it was something known and studied.

Well, I was in for a surprise. The days in the NICU and those that followed taught me that medicine is as much art as it is science.

All of the memorization, statistics, facts, and labs—all of the science, all of that—is just the foundation. The actual practice of medicine is passed on from one generation of doctors to the next the old-fashioned way: by the apprenticeship system of learning-by-doing.

Don't get me wrong; my children wouldn't be here without modern medical science. And there's nothing wrong with learning by doing. Generally, I respect hands-on experience most of all. After all, everyone rolls their eyes behind the back of the snotty MBA who thinks he knows how to run a company because he aced a few case studies. One would think that physicians, who acquire their most meaningful medical knowledge through the trial and error of first-hand experience, might have a sort of humility about them. On the contrary, many of the doctors I've encountered carry themselves with an aura of infallibility when they speak to patients.

Maybe this is an intentional attitude, meant to make patients feel better. Kind of like when you're a kid and things are going wrong, your parents make you believe that they'll do whatever they have to do to make it feel better without having to really explain all possibilities or their own doubts. But for a certain type of person, including yours truly, bold-but-vague assurances only make me feel worse.

As our stay in the NICU lengthened and the staff got used to us, I think I proved—to myself, anyway—that I could've become a doctor after all by cramming in all the knowledge I could. Between that, and my extensive familiarity with television doctor mannerisms (which is surprisingly a decent guide), I was able to speak to doctors in their language. And it paid off: I found that instead of just telling us about treatments and alternatives, medical professionals were more willing to actually discuss issues with us. It worked pretty well on attending physicians and some residents. As a rule, we found interns too enamored with the M.D. letters after their names to imagine speaking to anyone without them as equals.

⋈⋈⋈⋈⋈

I've been called many things, but shy isn't one of them and so I jumped into participating in rounds, and, thus, my informal neonatology residency, right away. I'm quick enough to hold my own in any conversation and blunt enough to say what I think needs saying. Christine and I were in complete agreement that I would be the point person for our children's medical care. As with any club, medical professionals have their own language and mannerisms and respond immediately and positively to it and negatively to "common" language. Very quickly we learned the lingo: CBC, stat, sats, PRN—you get the idea.

On September 12, 2008 we joined the conversation as the plan of care was discussed for Sofia and Daniel. It started in the same way, except now they mentioned Raymond in the past tense. But they didn't dwell on that because Sofia was doing better and soon they expected to try her off the ventilator.

Is there a cosmic balance that gave our two survivors an extra push? Did they respond subconsciously to the death of their brother? It didn't really matter because we were happy to hear the news.

A week after Raymond's death, Christine held Sofia for the first time and we both took turns kangarooing with Daniel. They call it kangaroo care because like a kangaroo, you take your tiny little preemie and skin-on-skin cuddle them against your chest and belly. The benefits to both child and parent are several, including

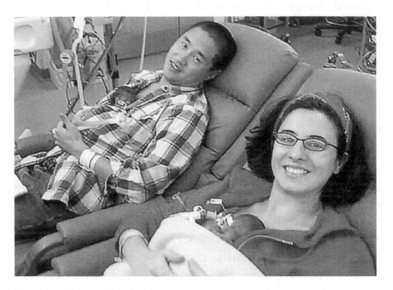

Kangarooing Daniel and Sofia.

stabilizing heart rates and improving breathing for babies, and bonding and giving a sense of control for parents. Our kids had the ventilator, multiple IVs, and a feeding tube, not to mention EKG and blood saturation monitors, so to arrange this was a very complicated maneuver. It's an amazing feeling to hold your child against you like that; they feel both strong and delicate at the same time.

Toward the end of September Daniel finally got to wear clothes—they were so small—and Christine changed his diaper for the first time.

There were ups and downs those first weeks after Raymond died, but they weren't dramatic. And finally, we were ready for the Sofia's first main event.

Weaning off of a vent is a tricky process and once the settings are close enough to natural breathing, the procedure is basically to try turning it off and see what happens. There also isn't a real definition of what "close enough" means; it actually is still a significant amount of breathing support. The process is gradual up until that point, but at the very end you can't be gradual. That's because in order to be on a vent, you have to have a breathing tube that goes down into your throat and that changes significantly how you breathe. The big event of coming off a breathing tube is called extubation. This is where the tube is removed, usually to be replaced with CPAP (Continuous Positive Airway Pressure, as featured on TV commercials with William Shatner) or other lighter forms of breathing assistance like oxygen delivered through nasal cannula.

Sofia had been briefly extubated in the days immediately following Raymond's death only to require re-intubation for surgery toward the end of September to fix a congenital heart defect, Patent Ductus Arteriosis (PDA), common in preemies. It occurs when a valve that normally closes right after birth doesn't close and results in mixed blood flow that could lead to major issues if not corrected. Daniel had it too, but ibuprofen did the trick, closing his up. Unfortunately, Sofia wasn't so lucky and they let us know that they needed to operate to repair it.

The operation went off without a hitch and Sofia appeared to handle it well, but she remained on a vent afterwards.

She was extubated again in the beginning of October. Her settings had reached a mild enough level where the doctors were ready to give it another try. Of course, I had my reservations, especially given our

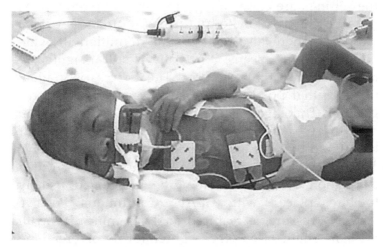

Sofia opens her eyes a few days after Raymond's passing.

recent loss, but they pulled the tube and she kept on breathing. It was amazing to watch her breathing on her own, even though she was still so tiny.

Girl preemies tend to do a lot better than boys do and this was starting to be true for our children. Sofia, who had dropped weight initially, was catching up to Daniel: she was at 1 pound 13 ounces and Daniel was 1 pound 15 ounces. While Daniel seemed content to discover his nose and hold it peacefully, Sofia was feisty, and prior to extubation had once pulled out her own breathing tube. We were beginning to see their personalities emerge from the various expressions on their tiny faces. By the second week of October both kids weighed over two pounds, yet we still hadn't really heard them cry.

For the next few days we felt that things were finally turning a corner, but our joy wasn't to last. Several days later Sofia crashed in the night, which required her to be re-intubated and put back on a vent.

We learned all about it when we called for an update first thing the next morning, although there wasn't much to the story. The doctors didn't know why Sofia stopped being able to breathe well enough on her own. Christine and I were devastated. For me, it was a bigger blow in some ways than losing Raymond. Intellectually I knew that this was going to be a rollercoaster and that there would be setbacks, but how ridiculously unfair was this?

Little did we know how much of a setback it really was. Sofia wouldn't come off of her breathing tube again for almost *four years*. Her damaged airway may, or may not, have been worsened by this emergency re-intubation.

CBCBCBCBCB

Are you seeing a pattern here? The course of care for our children was often like this: Progress followed by setbacks. What made it worse was the profound lack of data and lack of certainty about what was going on and why. Things went wrong, but could they have been prevented? Was a mistake of commission or omission made? Why? And was there any way to find out more real facts?

I am proud to call myself an engineer. I strive to make my thought processes as highly logical, rational, and fact-driven as possible. But even as I stripped away the emotional component (this was happening to *my* children!) I struggled with the uncertainty and my powerlessness. My participation in rounds and in those day-to-day decisions really didn't amount to very much when it came to it.

The traditional medical approach didn't help much here either. Although the various attending doctors quickly accepted us as partners in the process and included us as much as possible, the medical decision-making processes were far too experiential—and frankly guesswork—for me. The doctors did not tell us the filtered good news that most relatives of patients want to hear. Yet still these same doctors were extremely authoritative without enough (in my opinion) relevant data and with limited direct observation.

We were fortunate enough to have an ace in the hole that saw us through. I can honestly say that without Dr. Bob I would've driven the attending doctors and myself crazy with all of my questions. His advice led to far better outcomes for our children.

I called Dr. Bob when Christine had to go on bed rest in mid-August. When things really became difficult for Raymond and we were being asked to make hard decisions, I called him regularly to explain the volumes of jargon I didn't know as well as fill in knowledge gaps that googling could barely touch.

Dr. Bob was part professor, part confessor. I was able to admit to him what I couldn't even to my own wife—that I didn't know what to do and that I didn't want to have to make decisions. My life had always been one of choosing a path, then flying down that path and crushing it faster and better than anyone else. I was adept at following the rules when I needed to, but also at changing the game when I needed to so that I would come out ahead. That got me through the early part of my life in pretty good order, culminating in my Masters of Engineering at MIT at 21 and launching me on a career in high finance on Wall Street.

But being bold, smart, and brash doesn't mean a thing to your premature children as they struggle inside their plastic cubes. This wasn't the first time I had experienced a setback, but it was the most glaring example yet that I didn't have the answers and that I wasn't in control. Even Raymond's death happened so early on that it didn't have the same impact to my self-image and world-view as Sofia's first large setback. And, of course, there would be more setbacks to come.

Dr. Bob was someone I could admit my limitations to and who could explain to me in a way I finally understood that not everything was known or even knowable and definitely not everything was controllable. Not by him, not by our doctors, and not by me.

Dr. Bob gave me medical answers, but, more importantly, he taught me how to productively manage something I myself didn't fully understand and had little control over.

My epiphany didn't occur all at once and continues to have its relapses. But Dr. Bob started me down the path. For the first time I learned how to manage and accept a situation where I'm not in control; and it started with learning humility.

CHAPTER 4

HAVING AND NOT HAVING CHILDREN

"Sofia loves to be held but is still adjusting to her new situation... Daniel is doing well and eating a lot."
—*Yang Triplets Blog, December 30, 2008*

Have you ever watched the movie *Groundhog Day*? In it Bill Murray, the protagonist, goes through the same day again and again. He tries to change his destiny and escape this loop by making different decisions, but those decisions end up changing almost nothing.

Our lives were stuck in our own similar loop for the next few months. Our children *were* improving, but it was such a slow, agonizing climb toward improvement that each day looked pretty much like every other. We made many, many decisions about their care—from small decisions about their ventilators to more critical ones about several different surgeries—that would have been a crushing blow to other parents, but were now part of our routine.

We still called the hospital and spoke to the on-duty nurse at 7 a.m. before she went off shift. These conversations were usually a mix of technical details about the ventilator peppered with little anecdotes like "Sofia was really fussy last night" or "Daniel smiled at me when I changed him."

By 8 a.m. I went to work, and Christine went to the hospital where she would meet the new shift coming on and then sit by each of the kids' incubators, touching them and helping to change their diapers around all the wires and tubes and texting me throughout the day to let me know things were OK. Around midday, I'd call her for any updates.

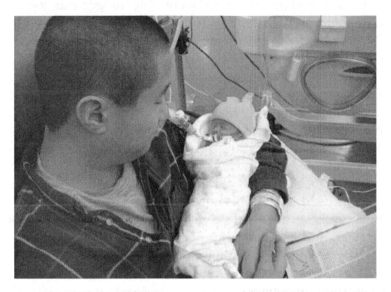

Holding Sofia in the NICU.

Christine couldn't focus on anything but the children, no TV watching or reading for her. Two or sometimes three days a week I, however, would leave work after lunch and go to the NICU and work from there. I was very fortunate that I could do my job just as easily with a laptop and Blackberry from the hospital as I could from the office and, more importantly, to have an understanding employer in Bridgewater Associates.

Especially since it was the financial end of the world as Wall Street knew it.

Remember the financial crisis of fall 2008? How the

Federal Reserve and U.S. Treasury came charging to the rescue after Lehman Brothers was allowed to fail?

The ground was shifting beneath our feet, yet "Don't Panic!" was the order of the day. Bridgewater, luckily, had a long-term view and a systematic approach and many of us were able to get our jobs done without obsessing over the markets.

The hardest part of my day (and Christine's) was coming home.

Having children was supposed to be an ecstatic, non-sleeping experience with a house full of noise—in our case, times three. Instead, we came home to quiet. No children, not even one. Each day we left the hospital emotionally and physically exhausted for our silent house.

The NICU was a far louder place.

I'm used to the noise of a trading floor, but I can't imagine how nurses do this for decades: the constant whoosh and beep and hum. They need to be listening for any change, a constant state of readiness knowing that a change in sound could mean life or death and everything in between.

A nurse was always specifically assigned to monitor our children and all the alarms were centrally monitored as well, but parents played a line of defense in the NICU nevertheless. This was especially true when the staff got busy or was pulled away for other emergencies, which happened often.

That first month in we jumped at every beep and alarm. Only after the first few weeks, did we learn which pattern of noises we really needed to pay attention to.

Out of all that noise, we learned to listen to one particular signal: the "desat." or desaturation alarm.

Normal people keep their blood oxygenation level

at or around 100 percent of nominal, but for kids on a ventilator, their target was to stay in the 90s. If it dipped for too long below that or dipped too suddenly, alarms would sound. This happened *a lot*. Simple, innocent reasons like yawning or rolling over could cause a temporary drop as could major, big-deal reasons such as a tube slipping out. You needed to be aware of each desat and what was going on as well as the frequency of the occurrence. If desats were happening again and again that might mean the vent settings (rate, pressure, oxygen percentage) needed to go up; conversely, if the child was constantly in the high 90s, then you might begin the process to wean them off the vent by reducing the settings.

So time continued to pass while our lives were essentially halted. We did manage to pick up a permanent houseguest in a stray black cat we found hanging around our house. We named him Truffle. He's a big fluffy black Maine Coon, and he turned into the perfect balm for us since we didn't have our children at home yet. We took him to the vet, found out he wasn't chipped, and adopted him.

Christine's sister Becky, who was supposed to have the first grandchild in the family, gave birth to a beautiful full-term daughter in November. While naturally I was very happy for their family, I was also envious of the "normalcy" they had with their newborn and the normalcy they would have going forward.

Other kids soon arrived throughout my extended family. Each full-term birth was another reminder of just how difficult and abnormal things were for us.

CBCBCBCBCB

November 21, 2008. Christine holds Daniel and Sofia together for the first time.

Sofia had started off way ahead of Daniel, but by the end of October, it was clear that Daniel was doing better. And while both kids had occasional infections, Sofia's often tended to be more severe.

Daniel didn't show steadily consistent improvement, as there were definitely setbacks for him, too, but the overall trend was positive. He came off his vent and breathing tube on October 11 and stayed off! We were finally starting to hear talk of bringing a child home.

But first Daniel needed a surgery of his own. It turned out that he had retinopathy of prematurity, which was one step before having detached retinas in both of his eyes, and would still require an operation to correct. This may be common in preemies, but it didn't stop us from worrying, especially since they had to re-intubate him and put him back on a breathing tube and vent in order to do the surgery. There was a tangible chance that it could go wrong.

This time, however, luck was with us and Daniel made it through the surgery, recovered quickly after extubation, and stayed on the path to go home. He even took his first bottle of breast milk, carefully pumped by Christine.

By mid-November, both babies were approaching 4 pounds. Christine gave Daniel his first real bath; I changed Sofia's diaper for the first time; and Christine helped the nurses bathe Sofia, which was awkward with all the various tubes.

November 21st was the day Sofia and Daniel met for the first time outside the womb when Christine was able to hold them both at once. Could they sense that someone was missing?

C3CSCSCSCS

Around this time, my mom came to live with us. We knew we needed help when it became clear that Daniel was going home while Sofia would remain in the NICU. My parents had been separated for some time and my mother had settled in Baltimore while working for our family-owned chemical company, ChemPacific, which luckily allowed her to work from anywhere. So we converted our still-empty dining room into an office and she moved into one of our three empty bedrooms.

My mother, however, did not come alone. She knew that she would be working most of the time, day or night (since she worked extensively with China), so she put out the call to find a live-in housekeeper.

For as long as I can remember, we would have women occasionally living with us as live-in "housekeepers." They were usually Chinese, often relatives, and always immigrants. When I grew older, I found out that my mom created these jobs for relatives—even once a friend's wife who needed a job to come into and stay in the United States. This caused no end of problems with my father, who was more inclined to see them as the help than as someone we were helping out.

This time, though, we really needed a housekeeper, someone who could do a great job cooking and cleaning. Jane was the sister of someone who worked for my mom, and both Jane and my mom showed up at our house late that fall.

It couldn't have been easy for Christine to suddenly have a mother-in-law and housekeeper—who only spoke Chinese—move in. We'd only been in that house for a year and a half, and between pregnancy, birth, and everything that followed, Christine never had a chance to make the house her own before my mother descended upon it—a woman who had initially not taken to my non-Chinese girlfriend.

My parents always imagined I would marry a "nice Chinese girl." My mother never said it outright, but she certainly implied that a Chinese girl would be more submissive and a better mother, able to raise a family "properly." This was exactly what I didn't want—and I'm not sure that the type of woman my mother imagined even exists. For the record, my in-laws never batted an eye at their daughter's Chinese boyfriend. Christine's family has turned out more like the United Nations than mine.

I was raised in an all-white suburb, and high school "dating" for me, on the rare occasion it happened, meant Caucasian girls. At MIT there were plenty of

Asian women, but I didn't feel I had much in common with them. I had wanted to be just like any other white kid for so long that I naturally gravitated towards white girls.

I supposed it was inevitable that I would bring home someone other than a "nice Chinese girl" to meet the parents. My parents were fine with Christine's half-Italian/half-German lineage (although she looks all Italian) as long as they didn't believe it was serious. Their anxiety grew as Christine and I moved in together.

Christine and I in 2003, the year we were married.

My parents were certainly always polite, but polite isn't the same as warm and friendly. My mother would say she doesn't remember acting that way, but I recall her being standoffish initially. It couldn't have been easy for Christine either in those early days of our relationship.

To her credit, when it became clear that I would marry Christine, my mother quickly warmed up to her.

I did make it known that I wouldn't tolerate passive hostility from my parents. They would have to get on board with my marrying Christine or not know their grandchildren. Little did we know how much we would end up seeing each other those first few years after the kids were born.

ⓈⓈⓈⓈⓈ

Like all Chinese mothers, mine was supremely confident that she knew how to run a household. After all, she was the eldest of six and helped raise her younger siblings back in Taiwan. She also had raised two successful sons. She is a very confident woman, and I get my confidence from her.

Like my mom, it's hard for me to admit when I'm out of my depth. I'm good at figuring things out or at least looking like I have: In any given situation everyone tends to think I know what I'm doing, even if I have no clue. And I certainly didn't have a clue that November of 2008.

My mom slid into managing the household with Jane, who did all the physical work. It was a relief to have one less thing like laundry to worry about when we came home from the hospital at night.

My in-laws visited every month or so and would fill in for my mom when she had to travel to China or Baltimore on business. Jane would remain at home, continuing in her role and I would become her primary translator. We appreciated the support, but couldn't always show that in the moment. We were focused on Sofia and Daniel.

To make matters temporarily worse, Christine had an accident driving my mother's car a mere month after my mom's arrival. It was raining and Christine

58

was on her way to the hospital when she spun out of control, hit another car, and ended up in a ditch on the side of the highway. Luckily no one was hurt. Unluckily, the car was totaled.

The driver of the car she hit was an elderly woman who walked away from the crash. More than a year later, and literally days before the deadline, she decided to sue us for damages. This was the last thing we needed! Nothing ever came of it because the woman died of other causes before any court action could begin.

The loss of my mom's car made it clear that we needed a serious family-hauling vehicle, especially given the equipment that our children might be coming home with (like ventilators) that needed to be taken with them everywhere. So as with everything else I do, I researched extensively and decided on a Volvo XC90. Now properly equipped with an SUV, we were ready for Daniel's return. But before we could think of having our baby boy home, we had a huge setback with Sofia.

CRCRCRCRCR

Things had been going relatively well. After her PDA surgery, Sofia was eventually strong enough for her breathing tube to be removed and she was tested for her ability to breathe without it. We were there when it happened and hopeful when we went home since all signs pointed to her being fine.

Things were far from fine, however. That night we got a call that Sofia wasn't doing well and had to be emergency re-intubated.

The situation didn't look much better in the morning. We found out that she was agitated and had difficulty breathing regularly despite the drugs they were giving her. She just couldn't stay off the breathing tube. Even worse, we learned that the reason she required emergency re-intubation was due to prolonged oxygen loss.

This wasn't the first setback, but it was the biggest one to date. Christine and I were extremely worried that Sofia might never recover. Thankfully, subsequent CAT scans and MRIs revealed no major issues, but her scan was "fuzzy" with possible micro-damage.

We learned later on that part of her brain was likely damaged due to a lack of oxygen during the emergency. That damage was technically epilepsy and a contributor, but maybe not the primary cause, to a diagnosis of periventricular leukomalacia, a type of white-matter brain injury. This, in turn, is likely the cause of her current disabilities and weakness on her left side. Her physical disability is also known as hemiplegia.

Sofia started to have mini-seizures several days after her emergency re-intubation—I remember the hospital calling us first thing at 8 a.m. on December 7 to let us know the first time. All I could think was: How much more did my daughter have to go through?

The doctors started her on anti-seizure meds, and were able to wean her off of them quickly as her seizures naturally subsided. To this day, we don't know exactly what happened.

We were now faced with another reality: Sofia would not be able to get off the breathing tube or the vent and, thus, would need to be trached in order to progress. Her airway was simply not sufficient for her to breathe out of her mouth and her nose. The medical term for this is floppy airway.

Were we completely surprised by this? No. In mid-November doctors had discovered that Sofia might have some airway constriction because they couldn't use a larger tube (as she grew) for the vent. But because nothing was definitive, we didn't dwell on it; we tried not to increase our anxiety any higher than it already was. Now we had to face the reality of a trach.

A trach is basically a hole in your throat through which you breathe, bypassing your mouth and nose; and of course it leaves the patient susceptible to a whole host of other problems. As for why Sofia needed one, there were several possibilities. It was possible that an emergency re-intubation may have damaged her airway or it was possible her airway may have been damaged even prior to birth, which then led to her failing extubation. Either way, our chances of bringing her home before 2008 ended plummeted.

When we first got the news that we were expecting triplets we knew intellectually that bringing them home might be a long journey. Our emotions had already been riding a roller coaster for months and just like that, it looked like our ride was going to be extended.

This was a *major* blow. Once again I found myself relying on Dr. Bob. He explained it this way: The surgery to put in a trach wasn't a major deal, but care and maintenance of one were serious and having that hole in her throat put her at constant risk of suffocation and infection. It could be months before she got off the trach, even years. Worst case? It could be permanent.

We still had a couple of weeks to decide whether or not to insert a trach—it was possible that her airway would resolve on its own. Meanwhile, Daniel continued to improve, and finally a date for his homecoming was set: December 15.

There was still one more bit of bad news/bad luck we had to go through before we could celebrate this:

Both Christine and I got strep, and we had to forgo days of visiting with our children.

About a week before coming home, Daniel was moved from the highest-risk NICU rooms to the low-risk room. Over the months of our stay we had seen many babies move out of our room—for both happy and sad reasons. Having gone through loss ourselves, we could always tell when the outcome wasn't expected to be good by the way the parents and the staff walked. Watching them wheel Daniel into the low-risk room, however, their body language and faces were all smiles.

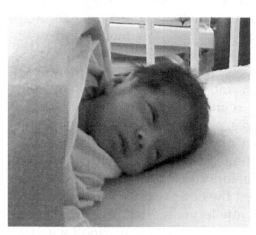

Daniel in the lower-risk room.

To go to the low-risk room, a child needed to be off any machines except the EKG; the babies in there looked like infants from any typical birthing ward. That first day some were crying, but most were sleeping like Daniel.

The staff immediately presented us with a checklist of what we needed to know to take our preemie home. For instance, we needed to have successfully completed an infant CPR class as well as have a car seat properly installed and a baby carrier—of course, we already had three. The nurses had us bring our car seat in and test it; they needed to make sure that Daniel could sit and breathe comfortably.

My wife wanted more than anything to be a regular mom at home, but I needed something more. It was strange for me to think that Daniel would go from being monitored constantly by machines to not being monitored at all just because he was home. So I insisted that he go home with his own medical souvenir in the form of a pulse oximeter.

Finally, on December 15th, it was time for the Yang family to bring a child home. I was overjoyed to take Daniel in my arms and filmed much of the occasion for posterity. Christine undid all of his monitors for the last time and put him into his first proper onesie. Then we took him in to see his sister and placed them lying next to each other, and so they could say goodbye for now. If they had opened their eyes they could have seen each other.

Grandma and Jane were waiting for us at home. It was a joyous occasion and for the rest of that day we celebrated Daniel's arrival. We called to check on Sofia as usual that night, but this moment was all for Daniel. At 5 pounds

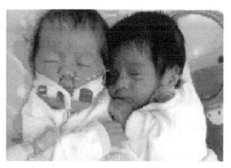

Daniel and Sofia together just before Daniel came home.

5 ounces, he was still smaller than many of my friends' children at birth, but he had fought for three months to grow and now he was home right around his original due date.

For the next two days we lived much like any family with a newborn. We took him to his first pediatrician visit to have his eyes checked, we fed him breast milk and changed his diapers, and we watched him sleep. We finally had a little taste of what it could have been like all along.

However, it wasn't long before Sofia's needs came to the fore again. She needed surgery for yet another common problem in preemies: hernias. They're common because their bodies haven't developed enough to keep their internal tissues where they belong. Since the doctors needed to put her under for her surgery, that meant the time had come for us to make a decision about having her trached.

No one could guess how long the trach would need to be in, but Sofia's doctors did explain that with a trach she'd breathe out of it rather than her mouth and nose and that should allow her lungs to develop and

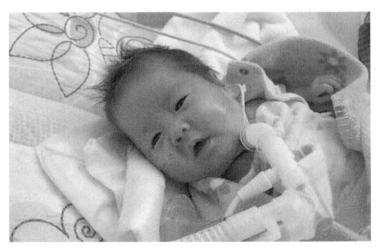

Sofia, four days after her hernia surgery with her trach.

for her to grow more quickly. Once trached and stabilized, she would be transferred from the NICU to a respiratory ICU unit on another floor of Yale-New

Haven Hospital. In that unit, we, as parents, would start to be trained in the special care necessary to maintain a trach so that ultimately we could bring her home. The best guess for how long until we would be bringing her home? Three months. And going home wouldn't happen until she grew to a large enough size and was either off of a ventilator or her settings were mild.

We made the decision to have a trach placed during Sofia's hernia surgery. The operation on December 19 went off without a hitch, but due to the extremely snowy weather, Christine and I weren't able to see her until a few days later when she was already upstairs in a brand new unit, hanging out with all new nurses. A nurse did email us a photo of Sofia post-surgery; it was the first time we saw her whole, beautiful face with its chubby cheeks.

She was smiling when we saw her with her new breathing tube a few days later.

❧❧❧❧❧❧

By the time Sofia left the NICU, she was one of the oldest kids there. That meant that we, too, had been there for quite a long while. Most children, even other preemies, were in and out of the NICU in a matter of weeks. Occasionally babies were moved to other units, but most went home after a harrowing but quick stay.

During our time there, a woman gave birth to quadruplets at 30 weeks—near full-term for quads. Her children grew quickly, moved through the NICU and were home within a month. I have to admit, I was jealous. Four? All healthy and home in a month? It just didn't feel fair, even though I knew it wasn't right to compare.

Other babies were less fortunate than the quads. An incubator not far from Daniel's held a baby on an oscillating vent. By then, seeing that, I knew right away it wasn't a good sign. Sadly enough that incubator was empty the next day, much as Raymond's had been the day after he died. There were even a few times when babies crashed while we were in the room and we bore witness to fellow parents going through hell.

Even though we shared a lot in common with the other parents in the NICU, we didn't really speak to any of them aside from greetings. The environment isn't exactly conducive to socializing. Because all of the babies are in one big room, we learned more about each other's children then we may have wanted to know or wanted to share. We respected other parents by pretending we couldn't see or hear what was going on, and they did the same for us.

ଔଔଔଔଔ

As a father, it was especially tough for me to interact with fellow preemie dads because on most days there weren't many around. Those that were there often seemed in shock to suddenly find themselves in the NICU with their premature newborns. Weekends were different. On Sundays, for instance, football games dominated the lounge TV and various dads would sit and complain about their teams, me included. But we never talked about our kids. Sometimes the conversations would naturally lead to talk about hometowns or what people did for a living, but it stopped there. Like them, I think, I wanted to cling to some amount of normalcy for at least a few minutes.

Looking back, I think it's a shame the hospital didn't do more to get us together, to get us to talk to each other about why we were there. Our backgrounds were often dissimilar, but we all had a loved one (or two or more) that we were caring for and could relate on that basis. It would have been helpful to compare notes. Instead it seems we relied mostly on our spouses, friends, and family—if on anyone. While Christine and I did build some relationships with the doctors and nurses who often cared for our kids, these were temporary. The hospital social worker spoke with us a few times, particularly after Raymond's death, but, honestly, I don't feel she helped me much.

I think the social worker was somewhat more helpful to my wife than to me because support structures in the hospital as far as I could tell, at least when it comes to ill children, are geared toward the mother. Even when we had our very first tour of the Yale delivery rooms and NICU when Christine was pregnant, knowing most likely our triplets would be there for at least a little while, none of the content was aimed towards dads.

Of course my wife was the one that was actually bearing and nursing the children and the one who was at medical risk herself. But non-medical support resources were also aimed at helping mothers cope. I didn't really notice it at the time, and it is only now with some perspective that I can see what was missing. Perhaps this is just an extension of the get-the-father-out-of-the-way attitude that prevails about birth in fiction, television, and film. Perhaps this was a result of caring individuals instinctively supporting the person they knew needed support. Or perhaps men simply don't ask enough for help. I didn't.

In retrospect, though, none of that was particularly healthy. Dads need real support and we, as a gender, are terrible at asking for it. And care providers should be more inclusive to dads, too.

Emotional support from friends and family also followed a similar, traditional path. Everyone always asked about Christine; asking how I was doing was more of an afterthought. People who knew me assumed that I was ok.

When I tell our story for the first time, I often hear, "how is your wife doing with all this?" The implication is that there is no way that a mother could possibly be ok with all that. That's a fair assumption because there is no way that *anybody* could be ok with all that.

Generally, I don't think dads going through crises receive the support they deserve. I received the support that I wanted but probably not what I needed. Would I have been responsive to anyone insisting I should speak with someone? Probably not. In the long run, what has helped me most is meeting other fathers at professional functions (as well as socially) who have lost a child.

We are members of an exclusive club and have more in common than we'd care to. Finding these fathers has led me to have a deeper relationship with acquaintances and business associates than I would otherwise have had.

Speaking with my fellow dads, I've learned we've all sought opportunities to not be the strong one, but needed the proper permission and safety to do so, and the best person to talk about that with was another dad.

What if during the commercial breaks of the football games on in Yale's NICU lounge we dads took the time to talk and get to know each other? Would that have helped us all get through our individual family crises? Maybe.

Many years later, my sister-in-law went through some serious health issues. I went out of my way to call her husband, my brother-in-law, and ask about how he was doing and if he needed any support. No one else had asked.

Dr. Bob was really the only medical professional I spoke with about how I was feeling. He was supportive, listening and reminding me yet again that I can't control everything. I guess it was enough for me at the time.

There are very few books about family tragedies written from the male perspective. If reading about me lets a dad understand that he is not alone, then I've done something good. If that dad then takes the big step to reach out and share with another dad, then I've done something even better. The more stories we get out there, the more we'll break down the silent-and-strong wall.

രുവെ രുവെ രുവെ

And so 2008 drew to a close, with Daniel home and Sofia trached. But there was still one more major incident on the last day of the year.

Remember how we had bought a Volvo because my wife had crashed my mother's sedan? Well, I had to crash that Volvo.

In my defense, it was snowing and my driveway is unique. To get to the garage from the road you have to go down, then up, right, and finally straighten out in quick succession. In the snow, I turned right too late and ended up on the edge of the driveway where it sloped up. The car lost traction and slowly slid off the side. Since there was nothing but air underneath the driver's side, the car started tipping over. In slow motion, the car flipped onto its back like a turtle.

Christine and I were the only ones in it thankfully and we talked to each other as it happened. "Are we flipping over?" "Yep." The roof held up like a champ and no one was hurt. Except maybe me since I couldn't stay put and banged my head when I undid my seatbelt. My mother, who was home, called 911 and fire and police arrived quickly. My wife waited upside down for rescue for about half an hour.

The car was totaled, Christine and I were bruised but OK.

Given everything that we had already been through, this second accident really didn't faze us at all. And a few weeks later we received some welcome news: The car was totaled and the insurance company was going to pay me *more* than we had paid for the pre-owned car. Needless to say, between that and the fact that we emerged without a scratch, I'm a Volvo-owner and State Farm customer for life; I promptly bought another pre-owned XC90 from the same dealer.

CHAPTER 5

UNEMPLOYED OR HOW TO RUN AN ICU

*"Having Sofia home is great! But it is still a big
responsibility and requires the ability
to react calmly and quickly when needed."*
—*Yang Triplets Blog, May 1, 2009*

It took us a while to get used to hitting the button for the seventh floor in the elevator to go to Sofia's new unit instead of the button for the third floor to go to the NICU.

Two units comprised the seventh floor of Yale New Haven Hospital: the Pediatric Oncology Unit was at one end and the Pediatric Respiratory Care Unit (PRCU) at the other. While both units dealt with children, the expected outcomes were wildly different. We saw the grim looks in the eyes of some of the parents we met in the kitchen and break rooms. As awful as things had been for us up to that point, we were thankful we didn't have to deal with cancer.

Unlike the NICU, which handled a variety of medical issues, the PRCU at Yale was designed only to deal with breathing issues—from lungs (pulmonology) to airway (otolaryngology, commonly ENT for ear, nose, and throat specialist)—in children of all ages, including teens. It was also much quieter than the NICU, which was often noisy and hectic. That was probably in part due to the fact that there were fewer patients in the PRCU and each had their own full-sized single-person hospital room.

Sofia had the same room for much of her months' long stay on the seventh floor. Off the elevator, it was a right and then after a few doors another right into her room. Just like downstairs, machines surrounded Sofia, but there was also room to spread out—to sit nearby and to work on a laptop.

A new unit, of course, meant new staff. We soon met Dr. B. who was the head of the PRCU and quickly got to know the various attendings and fellows who were there day to day

Nevertheless, the doctors soon learned that Christine and I were seasoned customers and therefore didn't sugarcoat or talk down to us.

In the PRCU, parents play a vital role. In fact, the goal of the unit was to integrate parents into the care of their children—and we were semi-pros by then. It was understood that many patients in the PRCU would not be going home with a clean bill of health and would need continuing care by parents, who therefore received training to do so. The training was done through lots of patient explanation and repetition by the PRCU staff.

Naturally, not all the doctors were patient with or fond of parent participation and the associated explanation and repetition process. There was one very young and brash resident who got her back up when I questioned her about Sofia's plan of care for the day. I don't remember the exact circumstances anymore, only her attitude, which oozed with "I'm a doctor and you're not." (Interestingly, I never ran into that attitude with attending physicians.)

We had far more experience with Sofia than any one doctor did, as Christine and I had been the steady witnesses to every event in her short life. Sofia's nurses also had more experience with her than the doctors.

Knowing this, good doctors weighed our opinions and didn't dismiss us.

I understand why the medical system needs to have a sharp divide between doctors and nurses, and doctors and parents. But doctors are, of course, not "better" than either of us. I think that getting into and through medical school instills arrogance into young doctors, and the residency system is designed to beat that out of them. Since Yale-New Haven is a teaching hospital that meant that we were inherently part of that process. I made it to med school after all, Mom.

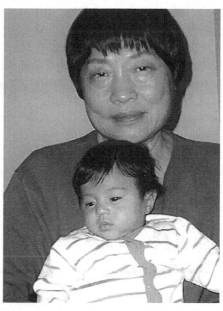

Daniel at home with his grandmother.

CʒCʒCʒCʒCʒ

I found out later that one of the reasons that the PRCU existed at all was because this level of parent training and integration simply wasn't possible in the middle of the craziness of the NICU, and, without a unit dedicated to training and respiratory care, children were staying in the hospital longer than necessary.

Many Americans these days have to deal with home medical care for an aging parent or as part of a fight against cancer or other illnesses. Part of the reason for this is the desire of people to be nearer to their loved ones and to remain in their own homes rather than in the sterile and impersonal environment of a hospital. But perhaps a larger reason is the sky-high cost of healthcare and the shift by insurers away from expensive hospitals into "cheaper" home care.

Christine and I certainly wanted Sofia home with us—and with Daniel. I knew that home care could never be the same medical-grade care she'd receive in a controlled hospital setting, but Christine and I were willing to do whatever was necessary to get her home. It was a herculean task.

First and foremost, Sofia had to do her part. She had to grow to at least 10 pounds and demonstrate enough lung and airway improvement to be on "minimal" ventilator settings. Just like when they

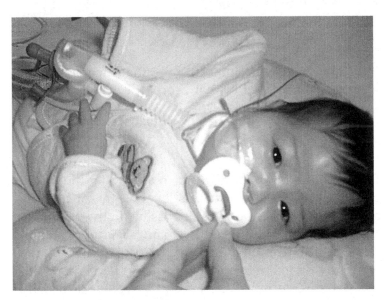

Sofia in the hospital, January 2009.

attempted to remove her breathing tube before, there were no hard and fast numbers so long as they were "minimal" and maintainable on the much smaller home/portable ventilators. She also had to show that she could weather general infections and colds without significant regression.

Having a trach makes being sick much, much harder because your nose and mouth naturally filter and humidify air. Filtering is done by the ventilator itself and humidification is done by another machine, but of course machines can't do the job as well as your nose naturally does. That makes trach kids especially susceptible to colds and magnifies their symptoms.

While Sofia worked to reach these milestones, Christine and I had to reach a few of our own. We had to be trained to monitor her 24/7, maintain the trach, learn how to change it in emergencies, maintain her equipment, and learn when it was appropriate to properly escalate issues to 911 and doctors. In short, we had to basically reach the level of nurses and respiratory therapists when it came to her care—and we had to speak their language.

It took months to learn everything necessary to bring Sofia home. Every piece of equipment had to be learned and relearned, every procedure trained and tested. We had to be prepared if Sofia's trach became clogged or her airway blocked—because of a mucus plug or because her movements dislodged the trach's position, for instance.

When that happened, Sofia would immediately begin to suffocate. The first sign that something was wrong should be beeping from a pulse oximeter indicating a desat or beeping from the ventilator indicating a pressure issue—but not always—and there are tons of false alarms. We had to know what to do if

Sofia began to turn blue and struggled to breathe. Since she was unable to make any noise, this could really only be determined by watchful attention. In this scenario, the procedure called for a quick trach change: You have to be able to disconnect the vent, change her trach for a new one, and secure it in place within *45 seconds*.

Those were some of the scarier scenarios we had to be ready for before Sofia came home, but there were milder situations Christine and I had to prepare for as well, such as when the trach needed to be cleaned, where a disconnected tube needed to be reconnected, or when simple alarms should be silenced or their settings modified. Changing the trach isn't necessarily the appropriate move in these situations. Judgment is called for. And every event required documenting it afterwards, contacting the appropriate people to let them know about it, and restoring supplies to the pre-event condition immediately.

For instance, I found dealing with her trach ties the hardest thing to master simply because Sofia would struggle and wiggle more (particularly as she got older), and there was always a fear that her trach could become dislodged during the process. We learned early on that it was best to tightly bundle her before we started.

Turns out everything we prepared for we experienced at home. Emergency trach change within 45 seconds? Yes, this happened. Too many times to count. A few times we even had to do multiple trach changes and go to a secondary backup trach of a different size. This is why we always had at least *six* backup trachs in various sizes ready-to-go.

Daily care of the trach involved regularly vacuuming it clean (while she was still wearing it!) and changing the ties that held it in place around her neck once a day all while watching for possible skin degradation or infection. In addition, we had to learn to feed her through her nose tube and later G tube (which is inserted directly into the stomach through the abdomen) and how to give her sponge baths with all the monitors on her skin. We had to learn to change the tubing on the vent, refill the water, and diagnose equipment issues. And we needed to be able to administer both her daily and emergency medications.

Luckily, thanks to my employer, Bridgewater, we had amazing health insurance, which included an unlimited amount of paid 24-hour nursing care. In fact, I played a part in negotiating the coverage at Bridgewater, not knowing that I was ultimately to become its number one consumer.

Daniel, Sofia, and Christine in our home ICU. One of Sofia's nurses is in the background.

However, 24-hour nursing doesn't reflect what you actually get in the home. At any given time, parents may be required to fill the nurse role because nurses get sick, call out for personal reasons, or cannot get to your house because of weather conditions. For us, it was bad enough that this happened infrequently— once a week on average, but it happened much, much more in the winter. Families without our amazing level of paid nursing coverage have to take regular shifts daily while juggling their work and families.

This then explained the intensive training regimen the PRCU provided. The final test was to take a full 12-hour shift at night in the hospital and act completely in place of Sofia's nurses. Christine and I each had to do that separately.

There was one last thing we had to do: prepare our house to be a mini-ICU. Not only were we to be "nurses" but hospital administrators as well. This included renting expensive gear, including two ventilators (one for backup), ordering durable medical equipment (DME) like oxygen tanks and suction machines, and, in general, filling up my basement with boxes of supplies. Insurance paid for almost all of it, but, of course, not without a fight, which was yet another task to be managed.

We received the bulk of our DME supplies from a single healthcare provider. There were few supply providers that Cigna, our insurance at the time, would support in-network. But of course, that bulk supplier couldn't supply everything so we had specialty suppliers. To deal with that for Cigna there was another, third-party, management company, whose job it was to oversee our spending on supplies. That meant that if a doctor ordered new equipment or supplies, we sometimes had to go to three different places to get it paid for. In some cases, it involved going back to those places several times.

The first time we needed any piece of equipment it was a logistical nightmare—as it was probably designed to be. It got easier on repeat orders, but often the amount of supplies we were sent would be wrong, the approvals needed (from doctors, respiratory therapists, Cigna, etc.) would be late or missing, or the reimbursement check would be wrong. Honestly the system is so broken that you would think it had to have been designed that way by some demon. When you are in a life-or-death situation with your preemie child, it makes very little sense to have so many players involved and expect parents to navigate it successfully.

Actually, it never makes sense.

Once equipment was sorted out, we had to establish 24-hour nursing care and coordinate an emergency care network and escalation chain between 911, our pediatrician, and the hospital as well as schedule windows for Sofia to be monitored by an army of medical professionals and, later on, therapists.

The only enjoyable part was that we at last had to get Sofia's crib ready and organize all the traditional baby accouterments: toys, rocker, baby clothes, which had to be just a little larger than normal to accommodate all the extra tubes.

While all of this training and preparation was going on over the first few months of 2009, Daniel was growing and being a happy baby—he smiled and began reaching traditional baby milestones like turning over on his tummy, albeit a little later than a full-term infant. He initially had some trouble putting on weight, but then caught his groove and started growing. In

March, at six months of age, he weighed 10 pounds and 4 ounces. Daniel had his share of pediatrician visits, but, for the most part, they came back with no issues. We juggled visiting Sofia in the hospital and

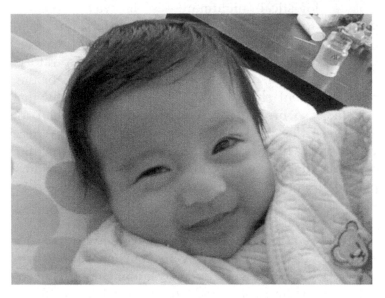

Daniel, March 2009.

taking care of Daniel—and I continued to work throughout this period as well, having returned to Bridgewater at the beginning of January after the holidays.

ଓଔଓଔଓଔଓଔ

Weeks turned into months and we got into the swing of things in the respiratory care unit. Sofia was growing and getting much stronger, smiling all the time. The first week of April 2009 Christine passed her 12-hour nursing shift and was officially trained. The following week I did, too.

Sofia's hospital stay in the respiratory care unit had its share of issues. She caught several colds and had to get past them. Due to her weakened lungs, these were an adventure we did not want. Her colds led to setbacks on her ventilator settings. Actually, when she was able to get a cold without having to increase her settings that was a sign she was approaching being strong enough to come home.

During one of these colds we also learned that Sofia's sense of hearing was atypical. A blockage was discovered in her upper respiratory system and ear tubes were put in. Sofia suffered a slight hearing loss and used hearing aids for many years. But I'm happy to say that somehow she moved past this and her hearing is now normal, even though we were told that hearing does not recover. Once again, Sofia was defying expectations.

But before she could come home, we had one more big scare.

A significant miscommunication at the hospital resulted in Sofia being left alone with her trach ties partially done. This is especially bad because the trach could have fallen out and she could have suffocated without anyone knowing since her monitoring was turned off. This was standard procedure for a trach tie change which happens every day. However, as we learned in our training, a trach tie change must always be completed and her trach secured. It turns out the nurse who was performing her tie change was called away on an emergency and did not get someone to take her place, restore Sofia to a safe state before she left, or even finish it herself later. We personally discovered her half-secured ties and turned off monitors when we came to visit her that morning.

We were fortunate; no damage was done, but it could have been disastrous.

I escalated the situation upon learning about it, quickly getting to Dr. Michael Apkon, who was the vice president of Yale New Haven Children's Hospital at the time. Several other doctors and administrators didn't seem to understand my concern. After all, nothing happened; Sofia was fine. Dr. Apkon, however, immediately understood that the issue wasn't just that something went wrong, but that the procedures allowed it to go wrong and didn't catch it.

There's been a lot of research about how checklists and procedures can vastly improve the quality of care. However, when they aren't followed or when things

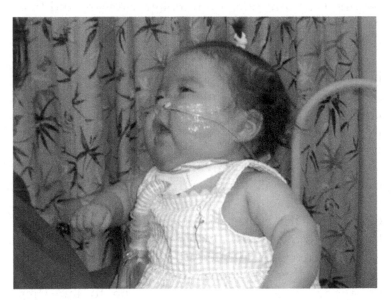

Sofia on her first day home.

fall outside of procedure, the gaps can be large and fatal. My concern was that it would happen again to Sofia or another child if a systematic diagnosis and fix wasn't implemented. Dr. Apkon and I were immediately on the same page and Yale implemented a checklist procedure for handling trach tie changes. With the scare thankfully only a scare, we finally heard the news we'd been hoping for: After almost six months in the hospital, Sofia was finally ready to come home at the end of April. At the PRCU when girls get to come home they call it, "Going Shopping." We'd been waiting for Sofia to shop for a long, long time.

Taking Sofia home was nothing like taking Daniel home: An ambulance brought Sofia home not our (new, non-crashed) Volvo. We had one of our new home nurses with us as we arrived as well as two ventilators, a pulse-ox machine, and paramedics. It was a complicated but joyous occasion that was long overdue.

When we left the hospital everyone was clapping and so were Grandma and Jane when we arrived—and I think Daniel, too. We finally had both of our kids at home, eight months after they were born.

There was no time for cake on April 28, 2009 as we quickly settled Sofia into her crib, which we located right in our family room. We chose to put it there so it would be easily seen from most of the house. A supervisor was there to make sure the equipment was all operating correctly and, before we knew it, Sofia was happily lying in her crib, connected to beeping machines, just like she had been back at Yale.

That first week I stayed home and we adjusted to our new reality. We put both kids together and played with them as a family as much as possible. We had to get used to this new normal—especially the beeping and noise at all hours of the night. We learned to sleep carefully, and I snapped awake whenever I heard a particular pattern indicating possible trouble. By reflex I would be halfway downstairs in a flash. There were no nursing shift issues that first week, which was great for Sofia and the transition, but not so much for Christine and me since we had to deal with the lack of privacy with the constant presence of a nurse.

Once again, this proved to be the calm before the storm, but this time, the storm came from a somewhat unexpected quarter: my employer.

CRCRCRCRCR

While Bridgewater continued to accommodate my working from home and/or hospital, not everyone at the company was cool with my situation—not surprising as being "cool" isn't exactly part of the "principles" the company operates on.

Ray Dalio founded Bridgewater in 1975 based on a set of principles about how to live, work, and how to succeed. I was in the first class of employee guinea pigs when he finally wrote his principles down and began teaching them deliberately rather than through osmosis and real-time, in-person correction. I was even featured in some of his early drafts as a cautionary tale. Ray's book *Principles* is now a best seller and my name, thankfully, appears nowhere within it.

Among those principles is the value of radical transparency and of constant conflict and challenge, which, together, allow you to get to the truth and make better decisions through a Darwinian process. It is highly unusual for a hedge fund to even think about these things, let alone try to run itself by them. The net result is that Bridgewater was and is a deliberately tough place where people are constantly debating all things with each other regardless of rank.

While the principles result in better answers, they don't speak at all about humanity or humility. In fact, feelings were something that needed to be overcome or avoided in favor of hyper-rationality. The principles treated everything clinically. Even personal failures. Personal failures, like any others, were viewed as something that could be overcome or worked around with discipline and effort.

At the time, my management style at the various financial companies I worked at could be summed up as overbearing. I led by being able to do the job that anyone who reported to me (or who reported to them!) did. I worked extremely hard and obsessed over data and details. I inspired my team with the goal of profits—or, at Bridgewater, the goal of excellence—and by being a personal example. I assumed everyone thought like me and drove them and myself relentlessly. I got my way primarily by being able to argue better and by having great results regardless of the human cost.

This approach led to great short-term results, which, in turn, led to extremely high compensation. That, of course, became self-reinforcing. Bridgewater knocked me down a few pegs thanks to its culture of challenge, but also left me feeling extremely confident in the things I knew I could do. It also made me even more blunt and overbearing.

Since the birth of my children, however, I was becoming less enamored with the status quo at work. Bridgewater relentlessly pursues truth, but in the process loses humanity. The obvious wealth at the hedge fund allowed some people to be generous and magnanimous, however, very small issues were pushed well beyond any sense and used as weapons for people to attack each other. It was an alpha-male, meat-grinder environment and designed to be that way.

Rapid growth (the headcount had more than doubled since I'd started there in 2007) meant that there were now many more people competing for the same prizes, and they were playing politics and using the principles to attack or eliminate rivals. I'd seen it happen before to others, and so when I came back from my week off while bringing Sofia home from the hospital, I knew that I'd stepped into something. A new "leader" was cleaning house and would shortly remove me and three other executives through clever use of the principles.

At home, I was beginning to realize just exactly what it was going to take to keep Sofia alive, and in the office, I was realizing that I no longer wanted to play what now seemed like petty games.

The tipping point happened when I was surprised (and also not surprised) to be accused of not being truthful over an inane thing: My specific crime was letting my boss think that someone that I was mentoring had suggested going out to a particular restaurant, when, in fact, I had made the choice and then didn't clearly say that to him or in my expense report. It's true. I made the choice and then didn't clearly say that I did when asked. It wasn't a big deal to me as my mind was focused on what was going on at home.

At Bridgewater, however, this was "Lying" with a capital L and a Major Offense. I knew I was being railroaded and could've stopped it—by falling on my sword (as everyone is expected to do)—but, frankly, the dichotomy of my home life and the absurdity of what I was encountering at work held me back. I knew where I needed to be, and while my pride wanted me to fight, I knew the better answer was to maneuver to an exit package that let me stay home and take care of my family.

I know now that there was no way I could've stayed working there—or perhaps anywhere—I would've quit on my own as soon as things got tougher in our mini-NICU, which did happen mere weeks later. Bridgewater had been very generous to me in compensation and was continuing to be generous through its medical plan and exit package, and I knew that, luckily, I had people there I could still rely on.

And so a little more than a week after going back to work, I was fired. Actually I'm pretty sure I fired myself since I had to prompt my boss to say the words and walked myself to HR after making my goodbye lap.

I hadn't told Christine how bad things were getting at work until about a week before my firing. To be fair, she had a lot to worry about and Bridgewater was always a stressful place. She was in shock when I told her I wouldn't be going back to work. Her first thought was about how we would handle insurance and her second was how we would manage without *any* income.

My pride still rails a bit at the injustice, but I knew where I needed to be. I left on Cinco de Mayo and the next morning I woke up to the sound of beeping, which was to become my reality for the next few years.

CBCBCBCBCB

To this day I don't know how we made it through 2009. We were always on edge, always scrambling to take care of something for Sofia while juggling our new family life. Jane took care of the cooking and cleaning and my mom watched Daniel when we needed to take Sofia to a doctor or back to the hospital. In between, we struggled to keep Sofia alive, especially when we didn't have a nurse. With less help and support, I honestly don't think we could've done it.

A few weeks after losing my job, we had our first major scare with Sofia. While changing her trach (a weekly occurrence), we were having issues getting it reinserted and she was struggling, so we called 911 just in case. By the time the EMTs arrived, things were already in hand, but we took the opportunity to meet and make friends with the team whom we would see a lot more of in the next few years—including Mike Handler, who was head of the New Canaan Volunteer Ambulance Corps at that time.

Sofia during one of her hospital visits in 2009.

In New Canaan, EMT and ambulance services were all free, which sadly isn't the case everywhere. Towns near us, some as wealthy as New Canaan, charged

$500 per 911 call, with insurance picking up all or part of the charge depending on the policy. The idea is to discourage people from making frivolous calls, but charging for 911 seems a particularly draconian and heartless solution. Since we were about to become frequent fliers, we were especially lucky.

The next EMT call was far worse. I remember that it was warm and maybe a bit rainy when we went to bed on June 29. By the end of June I was well trained in waking at the slightest sound, but our nurse screaming for help could have woken the neighbors.

The particular nurse on shift this night had been on duty just once before during the day, and she was not prone to hysterics or exaggeration. So when she started screaming, I literally jumped out of bed and ran downstairs with my heart beating out of my chest, knowing that this was for real. Christine followed me.

Sofia was in her crib, already blue and unresponsive when I saw her. At her size of roughly 13 pounds, it takes just two or three minutes for her to suffocate, so time was short. I snapped out orders for 911 to be called. Christine went to Sofia and my mom held Daniel who had woken up from the commotion as the nurse, having regained her composure, explained that Sofia wasn't breathing—her tube may have gotten misaligned—and the backup trach the nurse had switched to already wasn't working either. We put Sofia on the floor and the nurse began CPR as I reached for the second backup trach and then the third (we kept six nearby in various sizes and readiness) and inserted each of them in turn, trying to hold the trachs in place with one hand while at the same time pumping pure oxygen through the trach from our full-size oxygen tank that I had turned up full blast. I used the special vacuum to try to clean through the trach opening, in case there was a blockage lower in her airway. I was utterly panicked but somehow kept the would-be tremors in my hands at bay.

One-one-thousand. Two-one-thousand. Sofia didn't respond. Three-one-thousand. Christine watched frantically, thinking that Sofia, who had turned bluish grey without oxygen, looked so tiny and fragile.

The nurse and I kept at it—she with the CPR and me with the Ambu-bag and oxygen at the trach—as the sirens grew closer. Finally, after an agonizingly long time, Sofia took a breath and color started flowing back into her blue-tinged face. By the time I looked away from my daughter on the floor, the room was full of the people my mom had let in while we worked. A paramedic had a defibrillator out and started putting it away as he detected a steady pulse and reconnected her instead to the pulse oximeter. The nurse stopped CPR. We were out of danger. It couldn't have been more than 10 minutes since I woke up.

Our ambulance corps could only take Sofia to the local hospital, Norwalk Hospital. Christine went in the ambulance with Sofia and the nurse and I drove over on our own. It was close by and they quickly got her into the emergency department and seen by the attending. Since Norwalk doesn't have a pediatric ICU, however, the intent was for her to be immediately transferred from there to Yale. Instead, because the protocols were screwed up between the hospitals, that transfer took hours. We also had to go through many well-meaning staff at the hospital that asked lots of questions but couldn't help at all medically. Nonetheless, they did keep her stable for hours.

By then we had let the nurse go home; she'd done her part to save Sofia's life that night. Christine and I made the trip to Yale while another ambulance transported Sofia. We settled in to wait while even more doctors looked her over. After an x-ray to confirm trach placement, they announced that there was nothing wrong with her airway, or at least nothing more wrong with her airway than before.

It was morning by the time Christine and I made it back home. The next nurse thankfully had arrived, had already received the report of what had happened, and was cleaning up and doing the necessary paperwork. We were able to pass out as soon as our adrenaline left us knowing that Sofia was safe at Yale-New Haven Hospital and would be home again in a few days.

CHAPTER 6

SIX+ IS A CROWD

"Things are starting to return to 'normal' around here."
—*Yang Triplets Blog July 1, 2009*

I wish I could say those were the only 911 calls we had to make, but that would be a lie. Those two were the most dramatic certainly. Mike and the EMTs showed up a few more times in the next few years and not only for Sofia. Once they came for Daniel, who fell, cut his chin, and bled profusely. Apparently he wanted to get in on the whole riding in an ambulance thing. Another time my mother had a bad reaction to a prescription and I found her semi-conscious in the bathroom.

Sofia's calls were always related to issues with the trach, and, as per the procedures we had been taught at Yale upon her release, when she couldn't breathe for any reason, 911 was the answer, even as we worked to help her ourselves.

After the delay between transporting Sofia from Norwalk Hospital to Yale-New Haven, we established a specific transport protocol with our local EMTs that generated a minimum of downtime at Norwalk Hospital. Christine also created what was probably the most important innovation related to Sofia's healthcare: the one-pager.

The one-pager was a single sheet of paper which had Sofia's medical history, current ventilator/trach status, meds, stats, contact information for her doctors, nurses and the like. Whenever we met a new medical team (which was often as Sofia had many, many medical interactions with specialists and emergency rooms), Christine would hand them the one-pager—which she always kept carefully up-to-date—as a starting point. This saved a lot of valuable time, especially in emergencies.

Medical professionals would stare at us in amazement and disbelief upon receipt of the one-pager—not because we were so savvy about the medical jargon and not just because it saved the staff a lot of time in entering her medical history. Doctors and nurses would stare in amazement because, by looking at Sofia, they couldn't believe what she had been through medically, especially as she got older.

Throughout this, Daniel was pretty much a regular baby, crawling around and exploring while Sofia was confined to her crib. We brought them together often, putting him in her crib so they could interact a bit and see each other a few times each day, but it was awkward because of all the tubes surrounding Sofia.

One of those tubes was Sofia's NG tube, through which she was fed. This is a very long tube that is stuck through her nose and down through her esophagus into her stomach. The day-to-day explorations of a baby girl mean that an NG tube comes out of position quite often and getting it reinserted is far from easy. Inserting an NG tube means lubing it up and threading it down the nose of a screaming baby through her throat and down her esophagus. No matter how good we got at this medieval process, it never got easy. That meant that sometimes her feedings were irregular.

My wife had been pumping copious amounts of breast milk ever since the kids were born. From the beginning of the pregnancy, Christine planned to breastfeed. She did nurse Daniel successfully several times in the NICU and later at home, but stopped after Daniel developed thrush (a painful oral infection).

Letting the kids play together.

Christine did continue to pump, however, so by this time, we had a very adequate supply, almost filling the super-size freezer that I had bought for this purpose. For a brief period, while still in the NICU, Sofia had taken some breast milk via baby bottle—during those transitory times she had been extubated. But that was months ago and for such a short period that Sofia, for all intents and purposes, had basically never swallowed food. As a growing infant, Sofia needed more and more calories and nutrition, but because of the NG tube, she wasn't getting the nutrition she needed. By its very design, an NG tube isn't meant to be a long-term option.

We were reluctant to move off of an NG tube because it would require yet another surgery and, now that we were home, we didn't want to go back to the hospital—ever. And we also knew that if she were to get anything beyond an NG tube, it would be months—if not years—before she could eat normally. Hindsight is 20/20 and looking back, we should've moved her to a G (gastric) tube before we brought her home. Holding off on the G tube did not improve or reduce the amount of time before Sofia could eat normally: It still turned out to be almost *six years* before Sofia ate out of her mouth and breathed through her nose the way you and I do.

By summer of 2009, Christine and I were finished with inserting tubes down her nose. We gave in and had Sofia go back to the hospital for a very quick surgery to install her G tube. Of course, this was yet another tube that needed to be replaced, maintained, and cleaned regularly to protect against infection, but it did its job. Sofia started growing significantly faster, almost immediately. Sofia and Daniel were still not even at the first percentile of height or weight, but they were starting the long climb up!

CBCBCBCBCB

The rest of the summer proceeded in a blur. Is it because our minds try to shield us from difficulty— from memories of stressful times—that it's hard to recall details? I think so. How else to explain that even after looking at videos of Sofia and Daniel's first birthday party in September of 2009, aside from the cake and singing "Happy Birthday," I remember very few details? Christine, too, is hard-pressed to recall more than that. We were happy (the video attests to that), but also tired and relieved to have made it that far after our rough start.

I recall much more about the first anniversary of Raymond's death on September 11, 2009.

Up until then, neither Christine nor I had properly mourned him. Sofia and Daniel still needed us every

The memorial to Raymond on our mantel.

minute of every day and night. The first anniversary of Raymond's death was one of the first times I slowed down enough to reflect on his brief, but poignant life.

His life was cut off too soon. I never knew my son; he never knew me. My interaction with him was mostly looking at him through plastic, aside from holding him as he died. Was he aware of his surroundings? Was he happy in those early days before he came down with an infection? Did he suffer as the infection raged? I don't know any of those answers.

After Raymond died, we cremated his body and selected a small green urn to hold his ashes. To commemorate the first anniversary of his passing, we took some of his ashes and spread them on the hill in our backyard and planted a small bush nearby.

Sofia and Daniel watched from inside as we planted the bush. Grandma carried Daniel while a nurse held Sofia. It was somber and solemn—our own little ritual. I recall saying to Daniel and Sofia that this was their brother whom they had shared far too little time with. Of course, they didn't understand at the time. They don't truly understand now either.

Our idea was that each year we would set another plant nearby; we kept to that plan for five years. The rest of his ashes we kept in a small makeshift shrine that to this day is on the mantle of our living room fireplace. Next to the urn are a picture of Raymond, a cast of his foot and handprint, and the now-dried flowers and cards we received from our dear friends so many years ago.

The photograph could only be possible in the digital age. Other than after he died, all of our photos of him necessarily had tubes and sensors all over his little body. I turned to the Photoshop ninjas on Reddit for help, and they used their magic (and all of their skills) to create a photo of Raymond without all of the medical paraphernalia so that we could have a full picture of our son as he was in life.

Above his picture is a photograph of a bridge in Central Park covered in snow. This bridge was one of the first photographs we bought when Christine and I thought we were grown up enough to have artwork. It fits very appropriately for this solemn space.

෪෪෪෪෪

Summer turned into fall and the G tube continued to work its magic: Sofia's body and lungs grew rapidly. Despite all the steroids and surfactants that they dosed her with to forestall it, Sofia had a lot of damaged lung tissue by the time she left the hospital that spring. You can never really re-grow damaged lung tissue, so the hope is over time, the growth of healthy tissue overwhelms the old tissue. Because this was working, her vent settings came down, which helped push her lungs to grow even more tissue; this would continue in a virtuous cycle as long as she grew.

A fall walk in our neighborhood.

Getting sick, however, always threw a monkey wrench into our best-laid plans. Despite literally having gallons of hand sanitizer around as well as a strict hand-washing regimen, we couldn't prevent her from being exposed to germs: Having a hole in your throat and machines breathing for you isn't the healthiest way to take in air. Colds led to the trach being clogged more often and therefore requiring more suction. When Sofia caught a cold, her breathing sounded like she was slurping through a straw.

The first time Sofia got a cold was soon after her first birthday; it hit hard enough that we had to bring her back to the hospital. This is typical and an often-expected case for trach kids, but it didn't stop the incident from being yet another psychological blow. Again, we had Sofia in the hospital and Daniel at home. An intensive course of antibiotics had Sofia home in a week, but her vent settings went back up and this set us back by more than a month on the goal of ultimately weaning her off the vent.

As the weather got colder and we slid deeper into fall, Sofia was hit with another cold. At least this time we avoided hospitalization.

Colder weather, and especially unpredictable snow and ice, caused problems with nursing, too.

It wasn't uncommon to lose an overnight nurse because of scheduling difficulties (day shift absences were less frequent but also happened). More often than not, I would pinch hit and take a night shift without warning—I naturally function better with strange sleeping hours—letting my wife save her energy to pump milk and simply be a mother.

There's no time for dozing, however, as a night shift requires all-night alertness. Not only were machines beeping their need for attention, but Sofia's trach needed to be suctioned regularly and, of course, she needed to be monitored for any issues.

Twenty-four-hour nursing care was a godsend. I don't see how we could have had Sofia home without it, but there are plenty of families who are forced to manage without much nursing care at all. I have great respect for those families.

Every single one of Sofia's nurses was highly dedicated and professional. Most of them studied while they were on-shift so that they could attain advanced degrees, and many of them were immigrants or from an immigrant family. All of them were looking to better themselves by working 12-hour shifts, going to school, and taking care of their families—all at the same time. Just about every nurse had to drive over an hour to get to our house. They worked hard and constantly.

In order to be Sofia's nurse, you had to have an LPN degree (Licensed Practical Nurse—an associate's level degree) or higher as well as specific certifications for pediatric, trach, and ventilator care. One of the difficulties in finding nurses for Sofia is that many of the qualified nurses worked only with geriatric patients, which make up the majority of the home patients in our area. So while there was a large pool of home nurses, there were very few who could actually take care of Sofia.

Diane was with us for years; she was especially good with Sofia, or "Sof" as she called her. An immigrant from Jamaica and older than our other nurses, Diane, who had teenage children of her own, joined Sofia's team when Sofia was at her most fragile— just home from the hospital. She would regale Sofia (and us) with stories about her family in Jamaica and in the States. She would make Sofia laugh (and later clap along happily) every time she sang "The Grand Old Duke of York." I heard that song a million times:

Oh, the grand old Duke of York
He had ten thousand men;

He marched them up to the top of the hill,
And he marched them down again.

And when they were up, they were up,
And when they were down they were down,
And when they were only halfway up,
They were neither up nor down.

Unfortunately, Diane passed away, herself far too young, about a year after her last nursing shift with Sofia.

Sofia needed two nurses each day, every day. Our nursing agency did as well as it could, but not every nurse is cut out for this type of urgent case the way Diane was, and when a new nurse didn't work out or an existing nurse left, we would have gaps in the schedule that Christine or I had to fill.

Storms made this so much worse. Many of our nurses came from further away, due to the expertise required, and they would call out if they couldn't make it in or thought they wouldn't be able to make it home safely. If a storm lasted a while or we were unable to clear the ground quickly, we might be required to cover four or more 12-hour shifts in a row.

When nurses called off because they couldn't drive to us, Christine and I would trade off shifts. This would leave the house and care of Daniel completely in the hands of Grandma and Jane. Once again, I was thankful that I had the family support and wealth to enable this arrangement to be possible. But that didn't make it any less grueling. On our toughest week we covered more than 100 hours in total as Sofia's nurses when we wished we could just be her parents.

Storms also brought power outages. Sofia's life was literally in the hands of a machine that ran on electricity so we had many levels of backups. She always had two complete ventilator setups. Fully charged, each could last several hours with their associated backup batteries. Having two vents with her at all times (even for outside the home doctor's visits) was a must-do.

Then we had a car-battery-based backup system, which could provide another six hours of power to a single vent. I also had a generator installed in our house. Our house is electric-everything, including heat, so there was no way a single generator could run the entire house. The system we had installed selectively chose what we could power and where. But due to the limited landscape area nearby and the fact that I wanted a standard gasoline-powered generator, we couldn't have a permanently mounted generator that we could turn on by a switch; our generator had to be manually setup and enabled for every use. If we couldn't get her past a situation of no power for more than week, the next backup was Norwalk Hospital.

There were similar plans in place for oxygen, sensors and monitoring equipment, and trachs. Working this out, testing it, and maintaining it was a lot tougher than my final exam in circuits and systems as an engineering major at MIT. (OK, no it wasn't.)

CRCRCRCRCR

While we fretted about weather and the problems it could cause, Sofia continued to become stronger, and before year's end we were already starting to run trials with her off the vent. Doing this at home differs little from how it is done at the hospital: When her settings get low enough so that the vent is providing little support, you simply try turning it off and detaching it.

This was only done following doctor's orders and doctor-prescribed settings. Like the hospital nurses and our home nurses, Christine and I also had to be given

Christmas 2009 in the home ICU.

specific orders to change any part of her medical care. Some orders could be written PRN ("per RN"), which gave the nurse discretion to give her pain meds, for example. For vent trials, however, we were written specific orders for a protocol without the vent.

Her ability to stay off the vent started with seconds and grew to minutes before she caught a string of colds and winter hit full force. But even with the storms and setbacks, 2009 ended with Sofia strong and ready to kick that vent.

Ironically, it was as Sofia medically started to get a little better that things got emotionally worse at home.

Thinking about it now, that first year we lived in a

constant state of crisis. Unacknowledged birthdays and anniversaries came and went while we were subsumed with our single-minded focus on keeping Sofia and Daniel alive and growing. Everything was new and strange, setbacks were frequent and so were near-death experiences. Keeping all the balls in the air just for Sofia required being a nurse, hospital administrator, medical transport team, medical coding/billing expert, and more. Then there was Daniel, too.

By July Daniel was sitting up unaided and by the end of the following month he began crawling and eating finger foods like Cheerios. No less precious to us than Sofia, we nonetheless often found ourselves focused on his sister, dealing with urgent medical issues.

We had Grandma and Jane to help, but between them and the nurses—three relative strangers (at least initially) and one of whom didn't speak English—that meant there were six people (not counting Sofia and Daniel) in the house and often more as therapists, supervisors, and others came and went. Everyone was well meaning, helpful, and necessary, but there is only so long I could take having strangers and extended family around.

Jane, for instance, soon proved to have some strange quirks. She had been born poor in rural China and went to school during the Cultural Revolution in the late 1960s. Unfortunately, this meant that she was at an elementary school level since the emphasis beyond those years was on Maoist indoctrination as opposed to actual education.

Jane could speak a few simple English words and phrases and was determined to learn as much of the language as she could. She carried a notebook around in which she would write down English words she encountered and later ask my mother or me to translate. As a Chinese school dropout it was comical for me to explain more advanced concepts to Jane. I did my best to translate, but my Chinese is more of the "kitchen variety"—limited to words that we would yell at each other as kids. To Jane's credit, she studied every night and her English language skills improved each day.

Jane was a big believer in exercise and hard work. She did some gardening that was more like farming and grew very large and very Chinese vegetables in the middle of our yard—like opo squash, which Christine had never heard of let alone seen. (It did taste good, though.) Jane was also fond of flowers and once Christine had to explain to her that she couldn't just pick daffodils from someone's yard after she had brought a bunch looking too freshly picked home.

Gardening, cooking, and cleaning were not enough exercise, however. Jane started her own calisthenics workouts and one day a neighbor asked us if she should call the police because Jane was doing what looked like the bunny hop around our cul-de-sac.

Aside from opo squash, Jane was fond of deep-frying spicy Chinese peppers. This may seem innocent enough but was dangerous for Sofia with her respiratory issues. I am not proud to say that I found myself yelling at Jane in Chinese more than once while we opened every window in the house to release the oily, peppery fumes permeating the air.

This sounds funny now, but at the time it was hard, especially for Christine. She couldn't effectively communicate with Jane, who was responsible for keeping things going in our house, and needed my mother or me to translate, especially early on.

Living with my mother was relatively easy although frustrating at times. My parents had raised me to be fiercely independent so it was hard when my mother would do things her own way. But I didn't have time to argue and neither did Christine, who also was trying to forge a new relationship with her mother-in-law. We dealt with our frustrations the way people have done for ages: We avoided confrontations with my mom.

Except for that one time.

Stress levels were through the roof, my mom was doing her best, and all of us were tired. She was up late at night on conference calls to China. Christine and I were worn out ourselves, having been up late covering nursing shifts. Suffice it to say I said something particularly obnoxious to my mother in Chinese and she slapped me. I earned it. My mother had uprooted her life and moved in with us with little notice to help. She deserved respect.

Between having my mom and Jane constantly underfoot and then living in constant crisis mode, Christine and I rarely—actually never—had any time to talk seriously with each other. And when covering multiple nursing shifts, we wouldn't meaningfully talk to each other for days. Combine that with all of the stressful things that were happening and that meant a lot of bottling up was going on.

That's never a good thing. When the pressure came off a bit with Sofia starting the process of coming off of the ventilator, those suppressed issues and frustrations came bubbling to the surface. One night, Christine and I finally yelled at each other for a reason neither of us can now recall. We were in our room, on the opposite side of the house from Sofia, and I didn't think that we were that loud, but sure enough others heard us.

Including the nurse. We learned this because the next day we received a call from a supervisor asking us whether we were maintaining a healthy environment in our home. Christine actually answered that call and spoke to the supervisor first and then passed her on to me. I was clearly the "bad guy" in the agency's point of view, and, honestly, somewhat justifiably so. The supervisor explicitly didn't share details or name the nurse who reported us (even though it was obvious), and while she expressed some sympathy to our situation, she had to hew to the company line. The conversation ended awkwardly since, of course, we had to say that we would do better. It was embarrassing and neither Christine nor I appreciated their meddling.

Put yourself in my shoes. I am far from a saint. I've failed at many, many things, and keeping control of my temper was and is still one of them. But to never be alone, to never be able to let out your frustrations and just get angry at all of the unfairness around *in your own home*?

That's really, really hard.

It wasn't like my wife and I could leave and fight outside. One of us *had* to be there as a backup to the nurse. (My mother was not fully trained and so could not help in an emergency.) That meant that we had to keep everything bottled up, even as day after day we continued to fight for Sofia's survival while somehow living with my mother, our Chinese-speaking housekeeper, our son, and our nurses who, while part of the family, clearly weren't enough of a part of it to be able to deal with fighting.

I didn't take it well. Were we supposed to put Sofia in the safety of a hospital so Christine and I could have some alone time? We had to keep the environment a good one for our nurses, as Sofia couldn't survive without them. I suppose Christine and I could have tried to talk more (and we ultimately did). Writing these words, I still feel a bit angry at having been unable to express my frustrations. I'm not saying that fighting with your spouse is a good thing, but sometimes a little steam needs to be vented. Denying that isn't healthy.

I was duly chastened by the nurse supervisor and we got through it just like everything else. As Sofia improved, it ended up mattering less as our spirits lifted. By the beginning of January she weighed 20 pounds and was able to go much of the day without the vent. The doctors made the call to try taking her fully off of it for a day.

February 2010, right before Sofia came off the vent for good.

That day was February 6, 2010. Sofia came off the vent and she didn't look back.

This was a huge step for her, for us, and we were really, really happy on many levels. But it didn't change the level of

108

alertness we had to maintain. Removing her dependency on a machine meant fewer things could go wrong and that she was more stable, but she was still very fragile as her airway was thinner than a straw. Not having the ventilator and humidifier beeping was a great thing at night, but it didn't remove the need for constant monitoring. And the pulse oximeter beeped more than anything else anyways.

I let myself hope a little that we might just be seeing the end of her long ordeal. Christine and I began talking about finally scheduling the surgery that would rebuild her airway and let her breathe through her mouth and nose. Off the ventilator, Sofia was now ready for the next step.

CHAPTER 7

FIRST WORLD CARE IF YOU CAN AFFORD IT

"For the first time there is an open airway."
—Yang Triplets Blog, May 15, 2010

Do you ever think about how your mouth and nose work together to breathe? I never did. But I thought about it constantly after Sofia came off the vent.

An amazing amount of bioengineering has evolved in order for the mouth-nose system to work properly. Even more amazing is that, for most people, it all happens without any conscious thought. Aside from brief moments, Sofia had been on a vent and/or breathing through a trach her entire life. It was the only way she innately understood how to breathe. And until her airway was fixed, it was the only way she could.

Sofia's airway was stenotic—greater than 90 percent closed. Her airway was also damaged, either congenitally or due to previous procedures, and there was scar tissue in it.

Dr. Karas and Dr. Baum were Sofia's Yale-based Ear, Nose, and Throat specialists and surgeons. ENTs are the doctors who deal with upper respiratory issues, and they suggested she undergo either a Cricotracheal Resection (CTR) where the bad part of her airway would be removed or a more complicated laryngotracheal reconstruction (LTR) where they would take cartilage and tissue from around her ribs and graft it into the line of her airway. The graft would, in theory, strengthen and allow her trachea to hold its shape under the pressure of breathing.

Initially we had hoped that her airway might strengthen on its own, but after she was off the vent,

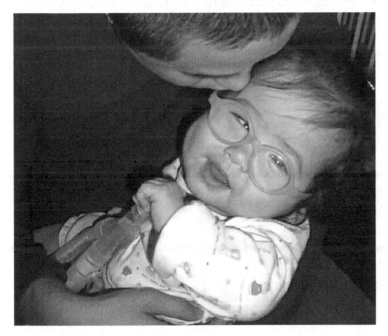

With Sofia, January 2010.

doctors quickly determined that that wasn't happening. Unlike her lungs, which were filled with new healthy lung tissue, her trachea did not repair itself as she grew. When they temporarily capped her trach tube to test her airway, they verified that she still was unable to breathe through her mouth and her nose. Surgery—an LTR—was definitely going to be needed.

An LTR is a multi-phase major surgery requiring 10 hours or more in the OR and a full team of surgeons, doctors, and nurses. Prior to surgery, Sofia had to be as healthy as she could be and large enough—so that there was enough cartilage tissue to harvest and so that there was enough trachea surface to which to graft that tissue. There is definitely risk with an LTR, but based on the cases that the ENTs had seen before, they were fairly confident it would work for Sofia. Knowing that the longer she was on the trach the harder it would be to come off, we agreed surgery was our best option. We didn't want Sofia tethered to tubes indefinitely.

Daniel and Sofia, March 2010.

Really the choice wasn't whether or not to do an LTR, but how extreme to go in terms of size of number of grafts, position of grafts, etc. So after consultation with Dr. Bob and finalizing the high-level plan, we scheduled her LTR for April 2010.

Sofia was still too young to know what was going on when we drove her to Yale that spring day. While she had been through many major surgeries already, those had been while she was still in the hospital. Now, for the first time, we were dealing with an intake process, filling out forms, and going through a parade of doctors and nurses, who checked and rechecked the plan.

After her initial exam, we met with every department taking part in the surgery: nurses, surgeons, anesthesia, and administration. Anesthesia would be one of the trickier bits because preemies can react in unpredictable ways to anesthesia—particularly with airway and respiratory issues. We spent some extra time with that department to certify her ahead of time and then spent more time discussing it further that day. We would grow to become experts at the pre-op process.

When they wheeled her away, I think I was more scared than the day she was born. This was my Sofia, whom I had held, loved, and saved from suffocating more than once. Christine accompanied her into the OR; I'm not sure I would have been able to leave voluntarily if I had. I settled into the waiting room with my laptop and a pile of books. This first time we were mostly alone in the waiting room, which actually had separate sub-rooms for privacy. There were some snacks, including the ubiquitous tiny cans of ginger ale found in hospitals and tea and coffee. On subsequent visits a kind person would leave baked goods, this time, however, there were none.

The wait was long and I found myself unknowingly re-reading the same paragraphs in my book over and over. Not superstitious typically, Christine and I dared not discuss our hopes, afraid of jinxing the surgery's success. After what seemed like an endless wait, which took all the 10 hours we expected it to, we were notified that Sofia was in recovery.

As it turns out, Sofia is not a typical preemie who responded poorly to anesthesia; she was very slow to wake up. When she finally did, Sofia was especially cranky, probably because of the pain of the procedure. And also because at her young age she could not

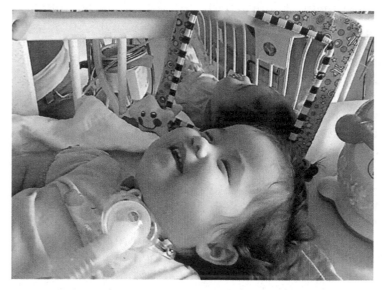

Sofia in the hospital, two days after her first LTR. April 25, 2010.

comprehend what was going on. We now know that irrespective of pain, Sofia is always cranky when she wakes up from a very deep sleep—like when she gets up late for school.

Dr. Baum said that the surgery went well and Sofia spent the following week in the hospital recovering before coming home. There she reunited with her old nurses in the respiratory care unit, who were very happy to see her. It helped us to see faces we recognized care for Sofia. Unfortunately though, it soon became obvious that the initial assessment was not as rosy as we hoped. Sofia's airway was not fully repaired.

This was later confirmed after our first post-op visit and scope. An endoscope is a big flexible fiber optic cable that is inserted into her airway so that a camera can view her trachea from the inside. Sofia would be scoped dozens of times over the years.

The good news was that her airway had been improved by the surgery and she was partially able to breathe—with effort—through her mouth and nose, but the amount of effort it required was not sustainable and, thus, overall the LTR was a failure. This was because her airway was unable to hold itself open, especially under pressure. Picture a wet floppy tube of ziti versus a slightly wet one. A floppy airway still lets air through, but not always because it cannot hold its shape.

This wasn't what we wanted to hear. It would take months for Sofia to recover the strength for a second LTR surgery. On top of that, Dr. Baum, after consulting with his peers, urged us to take Sofia to the leading center for pediatric ENT in the country (and arguably the world): the Children's Hospital of Philadelphia (CHOP). He could try again, but felt we were better off at CHOP, where he himself had trained.

That was a lot farther from home, of course, but, more importantly, to get her started in a new health center meant it wouldn't be a few months of waiting to schedule the next surgery—basically it would be another year. Another year of running our in-home hospital.

The news crushed our hopes and left us frustrated and lost in a way we hadn't been before. Would this ever end for our family and above all for Sofia?

I hadn't sought out support when we lost Raymond and still had two infants in the NICU. I hadn't thought to talk to anyone after saving Sofia's life on my living room floor. So when Christine admitted she needed more personal support, I realized I did, too.

We both made an effort to deepen existing relationships, which for me meant lunches out with friends old and new. And for the first time, we thought about joining a church.

☙☙☙☙☙

I wasn't looking to find meaning in what we'd been through via religion. I had started this journey without any formal religious upbringing and didn't find God in the process. Many people find support in their faith; it brings them comfort, acceptance, and peace. I wouldn't criticize anyone for that. But religion has never been for me.

I wasn't raised in a religious household. My parents had been raised in a mix of Buddhist and Christian beliefs that were more a house tradition than an organized religion. By the time my parents had kids, they didn't believe in anything and we never went to any house of worship while I was growing up.

Christine was raised and confirmed in the Reformed Church, a Protestant denomination, but lacked religiosity. This fit me just fine as I have always been strongly skeptical of any religion. While her church minister did officiate at our wedding, I asked (and she complied) that no mention be made of God or Jesus.

Our recent experiences hadn't really changed any of this. For a lot of people, belief, faith, and trust in God can get them through the darkest times and even make them stronger in their faith. In some ways, I envy that, and I will admit that at some of my low points I tried to make "deals" with whatever higher power might be listening to see my children through their travails. But that wasn't the same as belief.

I'm not one to lay my life into the hands of a higher power. Being told that a higher power would take care of things—no matter how well-intentioned—would go over as poorly for me as being told by a doctor what needed to be done in surgery without any explanation. That is, not well at all.

Our desire to join a church now was completely based upon needing a community. I was willing to live with some amount of religious content if that meant being part of a strong community. As it turned out, though, that wasn't necessary as we found a Unitarian Universalist church in nearby Westport that was strong on community without adhering to any particular dogma.

The way I see it, Unitarian Universalists are about equal rights and dignity for all. It's a church that doesn't require any belief and is simultaneously about all religions and none. Yes, there are sermons, but they're about thinking and asking questions, not about receiving answers.

This was exactly what I needed.

Christine and I didn't instantly make friends at the church nor did we immediately start sharing our story with everyone we met. That only happened over time. But it wasn't like we could hide anything: When we started going, we brought Sofia with her trach and her nurse.

Over the years our involvement with the Unitarian Universalist Church has waxed and waned. The church helped me ask questions I didn't know I had and put me on a path to answers I could accept.

ෆෂෆෂෆෂෆෂෆෂ

Aside from seeking out community, I also sought time for myself and picked up running again.

I wasn't much of an athlete as a kid. My immigrant parents didn't grow up with hopes of their sons winning the Heisman or even a youth baseball participation trophy. Studying, studying, and more studying was what they expected their children to do. My brother and I did that, but we also managed to fit in some soccer and later, in high school, I joined the track team. I was a passable runner—no hand-eye coordination required—but it wasn't really any fun for me. I didn't think of sports as fun.

I discovered the fun side of sports in college at MIT. (A tad ironic isn't it, since MIT is not exactly known as a sports powerhouse.) Up until then, I didn't grasp that playing basketball with a group of friends— I joined a fraternity full of athletes—could be fun, even though I am terrible at it. At MIT I also picked up running again and, this time, found that I enjoyed it. I would run on and off in the years that followed.

When I started running again in 2010, to say I wasn't in good shape would be an understatement. Over those first 15 months of our children's lives, we had no time to eat well, live well, or exercise at all. I barely huffed my way through a one-mile run that first day, but I kept at it with short runs around our neighborhood. Running became a way for me to take time for myself, to try to zone out of what was happening at home, and to actually be "good" at something again—even it if was only for 30 minutes at a time. Running became my respite: I came home tired, but in better spirits.

Reading to Daniel and Sofia in late summer 2010.

I continued to run for years afterwards, eventually reaching up to 50 miles a week (running longer as Sofia got stronger) in 2016. Then my knees gave out—first my right knee, then my left. These days I do less strenuous workouts, but try to keep it up. Overall I'm a lot fitter now and in better mental and emotional shape because of it.

CBCBCBCBCB

The disappointment from the failure of the first LTR left me examining many things I hadn't let myself look at closely before as we settled again into our new "normal." I was finding time for myself, for friends, and running, and Christine and I had found a supportive community. Regardless of our frustration over the unsuccessful LTR, Sofia *was* getting stronger and improving. It was going to be a longer journey than we hoped, but we were on a good path.

By the end of 2010 Sofia was taking her first steps and walking more and more—quite a feat with the tubes that had to trail her. Daniel seemed a typical baby by comparison. However, he was turning out to be a late talker, so we started him with speech therapy, available through a state-wide but locally administered service, Birth to Three. The program also helped with Sofia's physical therapy, which she needed due to her hemiplegia.

This would-be calm didn't last and again it was outside forces that were to blame. The economy was in the throes of the Great Recession. Even Bridgewater, the world's largest hedge fund, was looking to cut costs.

Through COBRA we had 18 months of our amazing Bridgewater insurance (with premiums paid out of our own pocket), and the state of Connecticut extended this time even further. I realize how fortunate we were that I could do this; so many face a far more difficult financial hurdle to care for ill loved ones. And 2010 was before the Affordable Care Act: Sofia's pre-existing conditions would've left her uninsurable if I ever stopped having healthcare coverage. That would have been devastating. Even if I could find other private insurance, there was no chance it would be anywhere near as good as what we had through Bridgewater. It was far more likely a new plan wouldn't have the coverage we so desperately needed.

When I was still at the hedge fund, one of the last projects I had before I left was systematically going to our major vendors—including those managing our health plans—and asking them to cut their prices. On that front, my instructions were clear. Bridgewater's Founder, Ray Dalio's, philosophy was that he wanted the best possible care for his employees in case anything ever was to go wrong. The cost wasn't as important as the fact that, in case of catastrophic events, the care would have no gaps in coverage and would provide extraordinary access to specialists. So while costs were optimized somewhat, no major changes were made to Bridgewater's generous health plan.

I had been part of the re-negotiation process, and now I was the largest consumer of Bridgewater's plan. Not counting Sofia's first LTR, the care for Sofia and Daniel was well over $2 million. Therefore, as the recession dragged on, it shouldn't have been a surprise that someone else would take a look at Bridgewater's medical plan and recommend changes to save costs at the next renewal period.

Those recommendations, when they came, were alarming. The current plan covered 24-hour-a-day nursing, which was vital for Sofia to remain home. The new plan would've cut this to the bone by limiting the number of visits drastically. We would've maxed out within two weeks. (This is the way most people's plans are, by the way; check yours and see.) This change alone would've meant I had to cover the vast majority of nursing costs out-of-pocket, which would've bankrupted me.

Our American healthcare system can perform miracles, but it is overly complicated and overly expensive. And unlike almost every other nation on earth, American healthcare is tied to the employer. I couldn't get other insurance without a job, and I couldn't get that same level of health insurance from another hedge fund with the economic down turn in effect.

I decided to try the direct approach and take my case directly to Bridgewater's founder. I had nothing to lose and we had worked on many projects together while I was there. Ray had drilled into me that he lived and ran Bridgewater by principles and so it was to his principle of providing great healthcare as part of taking care of his employees that I appealed. I emailed Ray and said that even though I wasn't an employee anymore, this plan change would be devastating not just to me but to his current employees if, God forbid, something should ever happen to them or their families. I didn't think gaps in coverage were what he wanted, regardless of the cost.

His response? He cc'd his management team, (many of whom I'd worked with) and said simply, is what Ted says true? If so, fix it.

Many, many years later I was talking to Ray at an event and mentioned this story, thanking him for the lives of my children. He had forgotten until I reminded him and was very gracious about it.

I know my situation is unusual and rare. However, the American healthcare system clearly isn't working if the only reasonable way out was for me to email a double-digit billionaire and ask for his intercession. It seems like common sense to me that the U.S. needs to simplify the system, enable real nationwide competition, and give people a baseline similar to what our federal employees get. Most people think Obamacare either went too far or not far enough. If you went through a fraction of what we had gone through by the end of 2010, you know what side you'd be on.

☙☙☙☙☙

Dealing with health insurance was bad enough, but we also had to worry about the power grid. In Connecticut, we love our trees. We love them so much that even though we have aboveground power lines, we let our trees entangle them—wind, ice, and snow can wreak havoc even in hyper-wealthy towns like Greenwich and New Canaan. It also makes our electric grid the furthest thing from resilient as *one* branch falling can affect neighborhoods.

Snow was plentiful at the start of 2010, but it was a freak ice storm in March 2010 that left parts of New England without power for days and even weeks. Up to 80 percent of New Canaan lost power thanks to ice-covered branches falling on power lines.

I had all my backup power-support systems ready to go at a moment's notice, but we surprisingly kept our power while many around us did not. Then, of course, our power had to be turned off so a repair could be made to restore electricity to our neighbors. The town gave us limited information about the shut-off plan—not nearly enough with Sofia's situation—so I marched into the office of New Canaan's Director of Emergency Management, who turned out to be the same Mike Handler who had been Captain of the Ambulance Corps and been a frequent EMT at our house.

Even with that connection, information was hard to obtain about how long this outage would last. We couldn't risk it being a longer time than our backup power sources could supply, so we took the step of

Damage from an ice storm in front of our home.

proactively bringing Sofia to Norwalk Hospital. Christine and Sofia spent two nights at the hospital before power was restored and Sofia could come safely home.

Connecticut, and specifically our corner of it, would suffer two more week-plus-long power outage events over the next two years. Both of these occurred around the end of October. This resulted in Mike Handler being the man who called off Halloween. Twice.

೮೩೮೩೮೩೮೩೮೩

By Sofia and Daniel's second birthday, we moved Sofia's home ICU from our family room to the living room, which gave her more privacy but still left her easily accessible to EMTs if needed. Sofia, stronger now, had far fewer machines around her and was more

Sofia and Daniel's second birthday.

sensitive to noise, so it was better for her and everyone else in the family to have her "own" room.

I was ready for a move, too—a move to working full-time again in finance—and Christine was ready for me not to be around all day long and start earning an income again. Like many moms these days, Christine had planned to take some time off, perhaps even a year or two, after birth. That was the plan with one baby, with triplets, she decided that she would stay at home for a while. I supported her decision.

I interviewed for a few jobs, including for the CTO position at another hedge fund, Tudor, but didn't get it. A friend of mine did get that particular job, however, and the COO asked me to come on board together with my friend as his No. 2 for at least a little while to help him turn things around.

I started at Tudor in December. The insurance

plans offered by Tudor were excellent, but they were not equal to Brigewater's. Luckily, Sofia had improved enough that we were ready to step down her daily nursing. During the day we would be on our own for eight hours, which left us with two nurses each day for eight hours or one nurse for 16 hours to cover the remaining time including the night. Tudor's health plan happened to cover just that amount, and Tudor was willing to be flexible if I needed to work from or stay at home with little or no notice. I could not have accepted this position without such insurance.

That left Christine as the parent primarily responsible for Sofia, the sole director of our home hospital and all logistics for the next nine months until my gig with Tudor ended (and we went back on COBRA), which was right before Sofia's second reconstruction in July 2011.

Going back to work started off being great for the family since I was able to get out and be meaningful again in my career. Frankly, I think it was good for Christine that I was out of the house, too. Though the paycheck was nice, in all honesty, my heart wasn't really into solving the problems of multibillion-dollar hedge funds anymore. And there was Sofia's second LTR to consider.

ᑢᑲᑢᑲᑢᑲᑢᑲᑢᑲ

My wife had grown up in the Philadelphia suburbs and it looked like all signs were pointing to that city as the next stage for Sofia's recovery. CHOP was an excellent hospital with a sterling reputation and we quickly decided that it was where we needed to look next, especially since our excellent health insurance covered it.

We happily found a familiar face at CHOP: Dr. Mike Apkon, who had been at Yale-New Haven Children's Hospital and was very familiar with Sofia after the tie incident, had become Chief Medical Officer at CHOP, and we were able to meet with him during our initial visits which also included Dr.

Christine and I missed Daniel terribly while in Philly with Sofia.

Jacobs, who ran the ENT department at CHOP. We had been warned that Dr. Jacobs was not the warm-and-fuzzy type, which suited us perfectly. I got along great with him; he was as direct as we'd been warned and always professional. Meeting Dr. Jacobs and finding Dr. Apkon there convinced us that CHOP was the place for Sofia's next airway reconstruction surgery.

Preparations began in earnest for Sofia's second reconstruction at CHOP in May of 2011. It was again an LTR but with a variant as Dr. Jacobs and his team would try a different approach to the graft. This time he also had to work around the previous graft that was only partially successful, but this wasn't an issue since he and his team were used to working with and around prior-failed LTRs even in extreme cases like Sofia's.

The surgery was scheduled for July and Sofia would be in the hospital for at least a week, maybe more. Again, the surgery would be well over 10 hours, and the recovery would take a very long time. On the upside, there was also a possibility that Dr. Jacobs would remove her trach if things went really well. Thus we had no idea how long we would be in Philly. Come July, Christine and I settled in the Ronald McDonald House in Philadelphia while Grandma and Jane took care of Daniel at home.

Ronald McDonald Houses around the country provide housing for parents who have to stay near hospitals that are away from their homes. They do this so that their children can receive necessary care. At CHOP, many parents come from even further than we did. Ronald McDonald charged a nominal rate each night for a comfortable room and provided free communal meals each night—as well as access to a full commercial kitchen for the residents to use. Those meals were a great opportunity to meet other families going through different medical adventures. In busy cities, there is often a waiting list, but we were able to get in without too much fuss. They are an amazing and worthy charity.

Our next 10-plus days in Philadelphia ended up being very surreal. Sofia's recovery was much harder than anticipated and Christine initially spent the first few nights with her at her bedside. After those first tough days though, she got better, and we were able to be more flexible with our time since we couldn't spend every minute at the hospital—especially as Sofia slept for many of them! We had one child recovering in the hospital nearby and our son was hours away. Neither Christine nor I had a job to worry about and we suddenly found ourselves freer than we had been—maybe since college! We explored the area around the hospital, known as University City (the University of Pennsylvania, which CHOP is a part of, is there), and even went out to dinner a few times.

The break was well needed. Especially for Christine, who rarely, if ever, left our home hospital for her own needs and spent every second with our children. I, at least, went to an office and was forced to worry about different things for some of that time. With near-constant worry over Sofia and concern about what Daniel was up to at home, it was harder for Christine to relax in the moment, but ultimately she did.

There is a concept called respite care which means giving the caregivers in long-term situations a break, a respite, from the weight of their responsibilities. Because so much of the focus is on the one who is sick, caregivers' needs are often overlooked or ignored. The longer the situation goes on, the more urgent the need to take a break becomes.

Neither Christine nor I had had any kind of break until after Sofia's first LTR. One of us—ideally both of us—had to constantly be able to jump in and make decisions at all hours. Even when things were calm and we had full nursing, there was Daniel to take care of as well as all of the administrative tasks it took to keep our home hospital running. My mother helped as much as she could, but she was working remotely at the same time. Christine and I did have some downtime during the night shifts as Sofia slept, but night was also when our major 911 incidences tended to occur. Was it PTSD? Eternal vigilance was the watchword and we slept lightly.

I had my first taste of respite when I was forced to be away from home for a job interview in California. Initially I was supposed to fly in the night before (Thursday), interview all day Friday, and then take the red-eye home. That plan was upended when the company's CEO wanted to meet with me again along with members of his team on Monday. So I decided to stay in Berkeley.

Suddenly, I had two full days that I didn't plan on. Of course I felt guilt that Christine was home taking care of Daniel and Sofia, but I, nonetheless, decided to make the most of my unexpected time off.

In California I rented a car and made plans to see Dr. Bob and his wife as well as two other friends in the area. I even visited a winery in Napa Valley. It may sound strange, but I enjoyed myself without the weight of the crushing responsibility of the prior 18 months dictating my every move and thought. And it was especially meaningful to hug Dr. Bob and let him know in person how much he had helped us.

I was refreshed when I came back and immediately jumped into running our home ICU.

Philadelphia gave Christine and me a chance to have respite together. We didn't fully recreate those first days of our relationship where we bonded over food and cooking, but we made reservations at decent restaurants and ate out, something we used to do often. More importantly, we talked; we talked about everything—everything except Sofia. We reminisced about how things used to be before we had children, talked about friends and family, and even debated English history, a passion we both share.

I may be an engineer besotted with technology and numbers, but I'm also a closet history lover. Maybe it's in my blood since my brother is a history professor. Or maybe it's because I read a lot of fantasy books growing up and thought kings and queens were cool. Christine was the history major.

November 2010.

Christine and I met in 1997 when she and three other friends ended up renting a room for the summer at my MIT frat house, Delta Kappa Epsilon, where I was living. She would be a senior that fall at Mount

Holyoke, a women's college a few hours west of MIT, and needed to find a cheap place to stay while working at her summer internship in Boston.

I wasn't supposed to be there. A trip to China fell apart at the last minute and I decided to stay in the frat house after graduation and before I started my job on Wall Street in the fall. It was the first time I literally had nothing to do for a summer.

I can't say that Christine and I hit it off right away. At the time we were both more into other people, but we did become friends and hung out quite a bit. What ended up bringing us together was cooking: We would cook together and talk about anything and everything. We both come from solidly middle-class backgrounds with families that immigrated relatively recently and instilled in us a strong work ethic, a set of values, and emphasis on over-feeding guests. (And we both love cats and walks on the beach.)

In Philadelphia, over a bottle of Chianti and a discussion about the War of the Roses, we allowed ourselves to remember who we used to be as a couple; we took those best moments and built on them going forward. We spoke about our frustrations, our fears. And we laughed. I think these times were the first true respite Christine had since our children were born. She never would have taken that time away from Sofia if the situation hadn't allowed for it. Yet, it was every bit as important to our relationship as the actual surgery was for Sofia's health.

CHAPTER 8

THE FINAL RECONSTRUCTION

*"We've got the kids home today to try to stave off any
illness which could derail Sofia's surgery.
That means it'll probably be a crazy day
with the kids bouncing off the wall!"*
—Yang Triplets Blog, October 5, 2011

Finally, Sofia was home, and brother and sister were reunited. Christine and I had missed Daniel terribly, but thanks to frequent updates we knew that my mother and Jane had taken very good care of him. Was it easy leaving Daniel behind every time Sofia had a surgery? Of course not. But at that moment, Sofia, and getting her breathing on her own through her mouth and nose, had to be our priority.

Sofia was clearly breathing easier now. But was it enough? The doctors at CHOP advised that we should give her a few weeks to heal and then bring her back for a checkup to see where things stood.

I had a feeling about "where things stood" and was fairly certain that this, unfortunately, would not be her last reconstructive surgery, even though I so hoped, longed, for it to be. Sometimes as a parent, you just know things. There's no rational explanation. This was one of those times.

On the bright side, things did get a little easier for the nurses and us. We resumed two shifts of nurses a day covering 16 hours right after Sofia returned. And because the second reconstruction had improved her ability to breathe around the trach, Sofia was that much safer on her own. This lessened the urgency of any issues that arose—and let us metaphorically breathe a little bit easier.

CRCRCRCRCR

We had a small birthday celebration for the kids in September. It was hard to believe that this whole adventure had started three years ago! In the beginning, we never could have imagined what our lives would look like at this point.

Reaching their third birthday meant that they had aged out of the state's Birth to Three program, and the responsibility for their services passed to our town, New Canaan. Therapists would no longer come to the house—we would have to go to them. That also meant that our kids would start preschool in the fall and receive services there. School-based care could last up to 15 more years.

Luckily, we were in a great district for it. New Canaan's pre-school program was an integrated one, with both typical and kids with special needs (broadly defined) in the same classroom. It was also fully free for special needs kids.

Still, this was a big step for everybody, and we worried about Sofia spending even three hours a day outside the house. Physically and medically she was strong enough, but providing care and dealing with possible emergencies outside of our home—as well as the exposure to outside germs—was a challenge.

First, we coordinated nursing coverage so that a nurse would go with Sofia each day to preschool.

Our nurses were all happy to do so. It was reassuring to us to know that a nurse that we knew well would be taking care of her at all times, and Sofia really loved her nurses. Why wouldn't she, as they did everything she wanted and were constantly around to play with her!

One big factor that made preschool even possible was Sofia's special backpack holding her "food."

Sofia the Explorer (post-trach).

Because CHOP was very concerned about acid reflux eroding any repairs in her trachea, Sofia was switched to continuous feeds and moved to an upgraded feeding tube called a J tube, which is a tube connected directly through an incision in the abdomen to the small intestine. The idea behind continuous feeding is that your stomach generates a spike in acid whenever you have a meal in preparation for digestion. If food is constantly introduced instead, then the level of acid should remain constant and manageable.

Sofia was fed constantly at a very slow rate throughout the day. At home, this was done with a pump that resembled an IV setup next to her bed, which had a bag that had to be constantly topped off with food. At this time, her food was basically a mix of super-enriched formula powder and mom's milk. Its taste was bland—like infant formula.

Clearly having a machine on a pole with her all day wouldn't work for preschool, so instead Sofia received a very stylish little black backpack, which held both her food pump and a small reservoir bag of food. This made her mobile like any other child and she loved it.

Sofia would have this backpack for quite a while, and it became another part of her incredibly large accessory kit: Traveling with Sofia meant taking with her a "to go" bag which had multiple trachs and the medical equipment to deal with any emergency situation. The bag also included a supply of medications and food in case she was away from home for an extended period of time.

Here's a *partial* list of what went into her to-go bag. We had one with her or in the car (with items changing as her situation changed) until she was 10 years old:

- 4 trachs—two each of current size and one size smaller, two ready to go, two in their boxes, trach ties, disinfectant powder
- Albuterol and other rescue inhalers
- CPR bag
- Tylenol, ibuprofen, and other painkillers

- Meds, meds, meds—she was on about a half-dozen at any given time
- Purell
- 1 can of formula / food and water
- Food bag and feeding supplies
- Two pairs of medical scissors in their own compartment
- Lots of gauze, tape, bandages, wipes, and alcohol
- Lots of syringes and tubes of various gauges
- Trach supplies and tubes, and, earlier on, ventilator supplies like batteries and wires
- Hearing aid batteries
- One pager and insurance documentation

The bag could get quite heavy. This was never an issue for one particular nurse—he was built like a linebacker only with even bigger muscles. We jokingly referred to him as her security detail when we met with the school for the first time. Nobody laughed. They thought we were serious!

Our district's preschool was held in one of the three elementary schools in town, West School, which was on the opposite side of town, and a van would bring Sofia and Daniel to and from class. The last precaution we took was letting our friends at the New Canaan EMT know where Sofia would be each day just in case they needed to "pick her up."

I imagine our first half-day alone with the kids at school was pretty much like anybody else's. We were anxious yet happy at the same time, and when the kids came home without any major incident, we were relieved and like any parent admired their "artwork," asked about new friends they made, and hugged them close.

This was also the first time since the children's birth that Christine was able to truly spend some time

Halloween 2011.

outside the home just for herself.

Daniel and Sofia were in the preschool program for three years, and not once did we ever have any problems. We owe a huge debt of thanks to all the nurses and the school team for helping to make that happen.

ය කකකකක

Soon after preschool started, one of our regular visits to CHOP revealed promise: Sofia was close to coming off her trach, but the doctors still couldn't say when exactly. Her airway had clearly improved, but she was leaking air around her stoma (the hole in the throat where the trach went in). It was possible that her airway would hold up if her stoma was closed off, but they couldn't tell given the leakage.

A minor surgery was scheduled in October at CHOP to repair her stoma and clear up some of the scar tissue in her airway. While the surgery did take several hours, and we had to stay a few nights, it was completely uneventful. It was no big deal compared to other surgeries we'd experienced with Sofia. This was a sign of how skewed our perception was that several hours of surgery and several days away were no big deal.

Once home, we quickly returned to our regular routine. At a post-op checkup a few weeks later, the doctors were so pleased with the results that it was decided we could start "capping trials" to determine if she could come off her trach. These are called capping trials because they literally gave us a plastic cap to put over her trach, cutting it off completely. This forced Sofia to breathe through her mouth and her nose. We had tried the tiniest amount of capping almost two years before, which proved helpful in diagnosing her floppy airway, but we hadn't really tried capping as a step in the process of weaning her off her trach.

That fall, her first trials were failures. The first time she capped, she struggled with the incredibly odd sensation of breathing through her mouth and nose. Of course it was odd and unusual: The last time she had done so she was a preemie newborn in the NICU. She thrashed and cried and was unhappy with the cap. But after some time, she got used to the feeling and we were able to keep the cap on for seconds at a time, then longer and longer up to a full minute as her strength grew.

Being able to breathe at all, though, was just the first, low hurdle. Sofia needed to be able to breathe *without effort*, even under stress, if the trach was going to come out. Unfortunately, after about a minute, her breathing would grow too labored for the nurses, doctors, and us to be comfortable, and we would stop the trial.

We kept with it, however, and Sofia made slow and steady gains of seconds at a time.

Sofia with her Passy-Muir valve.

We were also able to hear Sofia's voice for the first time thanks to a special cap called a Passy-Muir, which is also known as a speaking valve. The Passy-Muir has holes in it so Sofia could breathe in through her trach and, while breathing out, make sounds. She didn't have the strength to do that through her mouth and nose while fully capped.

Christine and I cried when we heard Sofia babble away. Could she make sounds prior to this point and did she? Yes. But this was the first time we actually heard her trying to mimic speech. She had a lot to say! We couldn't really understand much, but it was obvious that our little girl was highly, highly opinionated. This was a tangible sign that maybe, just maybe, things would work out for her—that ultimately she would be off her trach and able to breathe, speak, and eat normally.

With all of this progress, CHOP relaxed their restriction on her requiring continuous feeds, which freed her from the backpack completely. Now she was running around the house just like any other three-year-old, and she and Daniel fought over toys and played together.

Then came late fall and winter.

Our progress had been steady for so long that as the weather got colder and cold season started, we kept our fingers crossed that this winter would be different. We hoped she had gotten strong enough to stay healthy and make it through flu season. Unfortunately though, with her going to preschool, it was inevitable that she would catch a cold. When she did, it hit her hard. Luckily, we didn't have to go back to the hospital, but we immediately had to stop our capping and Passy-Muir trials as her breathing grew more labored.

She then caught one cold after another, and each one seemed to set her back further, making it harder and harder for her to breathe. Her half-dozen medications were unable to keep her healthy and stable. Therefore, it was clear that there was no way she was ever going to be able to come off her trach without yet another surgery.

Colds on a trach are horrible. Sofia had symptoms anyone would recognize: fever, shivering, stuffiness. Yes, her nose was stuffy, even though she didn't breathe through it! And worse, secretions had to be suctioned out; they couldn't be blown out of her nose because no air flowed through it. Secretions would get stuck in her throat and that affected her breathing. And when her breathing became labored she used more energy, which then made her intestines process her food more slowly, so her growing would slow, too—and that delayed future surgeries.

As the winter dragged on, we lost power yet again, but now were more than prepared to deal with it. Slowly but surely things got warmer and better for Sofia. We scheduled her third—and hopefully final—reconstruction for May 2012. This surgery would be similar to her second LTR except with even more tissue to graft into her trachea. The surgeons would take another chunk of cartilage from her ribs and give her yet another cool scar.

Sadly, Sofia had to go back to a J-tube (as opposed to the milder G-tube she had switched to) and go back to continuous feeds as prep for this third

January 2012.

major reconstruction. That meant she was back to having her little black backpack and we were back to filling a bag with beige fluid to feed her. She was happy to be Dora the Explorer again, but every step forward continued to have its two steps back.

Finally, May arrived and we brought Sofia to CHOP for surgery intake. We were fully ready this time to stay at the Ronald McDonald house and lined up everything required for Daniel to be taken care of by Grandma and Jane. We knew this was going to be yet another marathon surgery with a week-long-plus recovery period.

We saw Dr. Jacobs again, and he was confident that this surgery would do it; they would attempt to extubate her before she went home and send her home trach-free. Everything was set for this to be the main event of her life—and ours, too. She was the first and only patient that day that the surgical team would work on.

ଔଔଔଔଔଔ

Looking at the pictures now I realize that I don't really remember anything about the surgery. It was a very, very long day spent staring at emails and books I cannot remember. Unlike surgeries past, I stayed at the hospital overnight, too. I took advantage of the tiny little rooms available at CHOP for parents. Christine stayed by Sofia's bedside. Occasionally a hospital would provide a roll-away bed for the parent, but usually Christine was lucky to get a couch.

Staying with Sofia guaranteed a near sleepless night for Christine. Doctors and nurses would come in and out of the room throughout the night and Christine had to remain alert to advocate for Sofia. If Sofia was up, she had to be entertained and mom was best for that role. As Sofia got older and grew to love watching television, Christine was finally able to catch some naps while Sofia's favorite shows played.

Was it traditional gender roles that had hospital staff ask my wife first if she wanted to stay by Sofia's bedside? I knew Christine needed to be close to Sofia for Sofia's needs as well as for her own; there was no way I was keeping her from her daughter. Deferring to my wife's needs, especially in a hospital setting, was only natural to me. And I calculated that I needed to get enough rest in order to make proper medical decisions. Staying in Sofia's room would guarantee poor sleep at best, if any at all. It was very easy for me to fall into my comfortable and traditional role of being "the strong one."

Being strong in the face of adversity gave me a license to act tough because that was what a concerned Dad acted like, or so I thought. I took being strong to mean that I could be assertive and even dismissive with other people—especially when I didn't really want to talk about our situation with strangers. I'm sure my fellow parents at the Ronald McDonald House thought me aloof, especially those nights when I was alone.

As it turned out, it was a rough night for Sofia and Christine. Sofia was intubated so her trach was closed off and, as the sedation wore off, she thrashed and was uncomfortable with the tube down her throat. They had to up her sedation and painkillers to get her to calm down enough not to damage her newly repaired airway.

The next morning, Dr. Jacobs came by to say things were looking good. Sofia was under sedatives and morphine and still hadn't fully woken up from her surgery. We settled in for a long recovery period.

Once again Christine and I had a bit of a surreal relationship renaissance in Philadelphia. We enjoyed some nice restaurants, cooked with everybody at the Ronald McDonald house, and wandered into museums. We were more experienced this time around and knew the ropes of the house and hospital.

After this LTR, Sofia's recovery was definitely slower. She was improving, but remained heavily

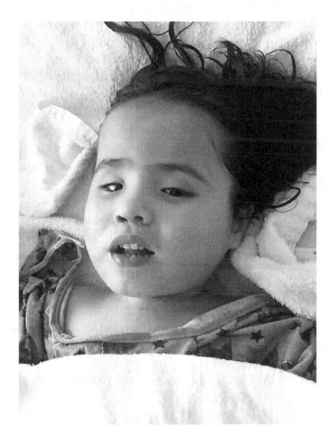

The first-ever picture of Sofia un-trached.

sedated due to the pain and on a ventilator because of the sedation. She also developed a low-grade fever, which thankfully subsided quickly. Sofia was barely aware we were in the room most of the time; we held her hand a lot and left the TV on her favorite kids shows. (Perhaps this is why even now she is still addicted to the same shows?)

A few days into her recovery, Sofia was taken into the OR and scoped so the doctors could see how her airway looked. We were relieved to hear that all looked well and the doctors could soon attempt an extubation. They would not wake her up first because her agitation might damage things. The plan, therefore, was to slowly reduce her sedation, cut the vent so that she could breathe on her own again, and then pull the tube and basically see what happens.

We were there early that morning, Tuesday, May 12, 2012. The sun was shining and the room was packed with doctors and nurses as Dr. Jacobs prepared to extubate Sofia.

Without any fanfare, he did it. We watched from the foot of the bed, close enough to touch her if we wanted to but out of the way of the doctors and nurses.

Sofia seemed to breathe fine initially, but then grew more agitated and snapped fully awake. She was clearly in pain as she took in air through her mouth and nose without any breathing support.

It was agonizing to watch her suffer, but a room full of medical professionals was standing by, prepared to intervene if necessary. I had hoped she would be able to handle breathing on her own and now I was watching her struggle and gasp for breath. The minutes slowly ticked by with little to no improvement. Our faith wavered. Oxygen support was provided to Sofia and as the minutes became hours and ultimately days, she improved and grew stronger. As her breathing eased, they backed off oxygen support little by little until she was on regular room air. And then, finally, she comfortably breathed just like any other child. It was our miracle. It was the first real prolonged time she had done this in her life, and it was beautiful to watch her smile and breathe easily.

Before we could go home, however, there was one more unexpected hurdle. In order to keep her sedated, Sofia had been on a very heavy dose of morphine and other opioids for more than a week. Thus, it wasn't long after extubation when Sofia started to go through the symptoms of withdrawal. The doctors were expecting it, but, for us, watching her shiver, shake, and flail in phantom pain was impossible to bear, especially hours after watching her gasp for breath. They restarted some of the opioids to ease her pain and it took a few more days in the hospital to wean her off them.

Finally though, after 16 long days in the hospital, we were able to bring our trach-free girl home to her brother!

CHAPTER 9

PAYING THE BILLS OR EVERYTHING I LEARNED ABOUT ENTREPRENEURSHIP I LEARNED FROM MY PREEMIES

*"And my special reward for all this progress
is to return to work tomorrow."*
—*Yang Triplets Blog, September 8, 2008*

It was more than four years after her birth before Sofia could breathe the way you and I take for granted. It was four years before we heard her giggle; four years before we had a photo of her without any machinery connected to her body. It was important for me—as it would be for any father—that I was there every step of the journey.

I realize I was luckier than most in that I *could* be there: I didn't have to work two (or three) jobs to cover medical costs; I didn't struggle with finding, keeping, and paying for good insurance; and my children received the best possible care inside and outside of hospitals. I was focused on Sofia, on just trying to keep my daughter alive, and I don't think my brain or my body could have handled the 70-plus-hour-long workweeks that were once my norm.

Who am I kidding? I *know* that there is no way I could have worked full-time during much of these first five years of Sofia and Daniel's lives; home was where I needed and wanted to be.

Ironically, I received a lot of calls from headhunters soon after I left Bridgewater in May 2009, and some of those led to part-time consulting gigs. But I couldn't really focus on anything other than the care of my family. I was lucky to have exceptional health insurance and to have banked enough money to not need to work—most people don't have these advantages. Most parents of preemies, especially those with long-term needs, precariously juggle care while working.

I didn't work full-time again until I returned to the hedge fund world at Tudor, which was after Daniel

How could I not have been with Sofia at the hospital?

and Sofia's second birthday in late 2010. Sofia was stable enough after her first LTR to make thinking about work possible, so I naturally thought about resuming my career where it left off.

In retrospect, my search for another Chief Technology Officer slot could only have ended in failure: I lacked enthusiasm for solving the same problems again and the time and travel commitment needed were still overwhelming. Still, I launched into my search with the best intentions. I was focused on earning a living the way I knew how. From the vantage point of a few years, I can say that so much of my ego was tied into my job and my title that I needed to get those offers to offset all the turmoil happening at home. But that turmoil at home had redefined me.

I've always had an entrepreneurial streak, which started long before the triplets were born. I bailed out of JP Morgan during the Web 1.0 days in 1999 to found my first startup, eTechtransfer with five other like-minded entrepreneurs. It crashed and burned spectacularly, but not without winning the prestigious Wharton Business Plan Competition of 2000. I always say that that was the worst thing that happened to us. It led a bunch of twenty-somethings into thinking that they knew what they were doing. We did not. If you really want to you might be able to google and figure out what we did. If you do let me know, because one of our problems was that we never quite figured it out ourselves!

I went back with my tail between my legs to work on Wall Street but didn't completely give up on starting companies. I was a well-paid servant of various financial masters, but I found time to help launch and be a founding investor of two companies, both of which have gone through some very rough patches but are still around, growing, and doing well. I still sit on their boards.

Being on a board, though, means that barring major emergencies and a few meetings a year, my role is limited. Thus when a friend approached me with an idea for a startup in 2010, even though I wasn't fully ready for full-time work again, I was excited. The idea was a sound one: to be the "Lending Tree" for 401k rollovers; we called it IRAMarket. This was my chance to do something I enjoy and have discovered I do well: build and manage a company.

This was the first of three companies I ultimately founded with a partner named Bill. Interestingly I had invested some money with this particular Bill in an earlier venture of his that didn't succeed. That, of course, didn't stop me.

IRAmarket had early success, raised seed capital, and then went live with our offering with Prudential as a partner. We ultimately hit a wall, however, because investment companies insisted on paper signatures to complete a rollover. Imagine doing everything online only to have to print out, fill out, and fax in a sheaf of documents to finalize your rollover! To deal with that, we ultimately partnered with and then sold IRAmarket to a company that was already fighting the massive legal and regulatory inertia around moving to fully electronic rollovers, which now, of course, are ordinary.

All of this happened before things got rolling for me full-time at Tudor in 2010. My time as an entrepreneur clearly colored my thinking about full-time work. After what had happened with Sofia and while she was still on her trach, it became obvious to me that bringing in a salary while working for someone else, no matter how highly compensated and how nice the fringe benefits, wasn't something that I was motivated to do—and overall wasn't worth it.

The problems that I had enjoyed solving for so long in finance were boring and uninteresting to me now.

When you hold your daughter's life in your hands, making numbers dance the way you want them to lacks appeal—forget about all the politics and squabbling. I also wanted to be able to set my own clock and be with my family when I needed to be.

Yes, I was still a little naïve about the control and flexibility that you have as an entrepreneur. Spoiler alert: You actually have little to none. An entrepreneur has many, many bosses. She works for her customers,

Daniel, June 2012.

investors, partners, and also her employees, who if they left, would crash the company. Just reporting to a single boss is vastly easier, but not nearly as fulfilling.

When you get senior enough as a corporate minion, your skills become less translatable and the jobs you are suited for become increasingly narrow. I know this is somewhat confusing to hear because people like to think that their careers open horizons. But the opposite is true: You become super-specialized at what you do. Furthermore, companies love predictability and pay you a lot of money to do basically exactly what you've done before; they don't pay you to jump into doing anything new, despite all rhetoric to the contrary about "innovation" and "taking risks."

The money I had made was addicting, but no one really *needs* that kind of money. Christine and I had always been frugal and never spent more than a

Sofia, June 2012.

fraction of the money that we made. I credit this completely to our parents. Mine grew up as refugees from WWII. Both my parents had to restart their lives in Taiwan after fleeing from the communists who took over China; they literally grew up dirt poor. And then they had to restart again as young adults in America once they were able to accumulate enough education to get in.

I never knew my grandparents well. My father's parents lived in Vancouver and while we dutifully visited every two years, that wasn't enough to build any relationship with them. My mother's parents ultimately lived down the road from us for a few years, but with my limited Mandarin and their limited English, our conversations were mostly about food and studying.

My maternal grandfather taught himself English and eventually told me a few stories about his past and that he had been in the Chinese Nationalist Army. After he died at 100, I learned he wasn't a foot soldier, as I had always been led to believe, but a two-star general and ultimately Chief Quartermaster for Taiwan. He had been one of the youngest generals in the Army. Wait, how could your grandfather have been Chief Quartermaster and yet your mother grew up poor? Simple answer. His predecessor was shot for corruption and theft.

My wife's parents grew up with modest means and both became teachers. They always put doing the right thing far, far ahead of their own monetary gain.

Christine and I never leaned into the Connecticut big-finance lifestyle, but we had gotten used to having excess money around. The shock of going from two incomes to almost none was a big one. Neither one of us worked for almost 18 months—and, again, I know most people can't do this. Though with Sofia and Daniel needing round-the-clock care, we had little to spend money on anyway.

The fact that we survived that shock meant that as I returned to work, I had a much higher tolerance for unpredictable income than I previously did. This is the first major thing I learned from my preemies about being an entrepreneur: I can live with unpredictable income and risk.

What's a little financial risk compared to the risks we took to have Sofia breathe on her own?

Collecting a check from a corporation is easy; most companies will be around for longer than you will work there. But when it is your own company setbacks are inevitable, especially early on. Even if things go well for periods of time, they may turn. And if you are growing fast, you will have little to no retained earnings, which means having to cut your own pay when times are bad so that your employees are taken care of and paying yourself last when times are good.

I knew I couldn't be a CTO at a big financial firm anymore and was ready to take some risk in my paycheck, but I didn't know what I wanted to be instead. I had plenty of energy, drive, and hunger left, just not for finance. I guess at the time I still thought I could found that next billion-dollar company, which is why I jumped into IRAmarket. But to be honest, I was never all-in with IRAmarket despite being a co-founder. That was because Sofia wasn't all that stable. I worked when I could, where I could.

෬෬෬෬෬෬

By 2012, two LTRs in, Sofia *was* stable enough for me to try going all-in as an entrepreneur. But I couldn't find an opportunity that really appealed, partly because I wanted to be close and nearby in Connecticut.

Needing to explore more, I joined an angel investor group and had fun funding local startups that I shouldn't have invested in. I enjoyed the group for the networking and made a few friendships that I've maintained since. Being an angel investor was flexible, sometimes interesting, and I learned some brand new skills, but it was no way to make a living.

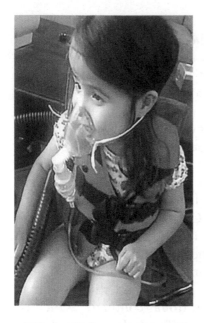

Sofia is off her trach, but still needs help to clear her airway.

While I was able to be there for and with Sofia, I wasn't bringing in any real money—quite the opposite, in fact, as I was putting it into various small startups, most of which, of course, went nowhere.

The core problem was that there weren't enough *quality* startups. This is always an issue, but a decade ago, there was no such thing as an entrepreneurial ecosystem in Connecticut like you would find in Silicon Valley, Silicon Alley, or Boston. Connecticut didn't even have a co-working space or entrepreneur educational programs and certainly did not have a strong startup incubator. We were rapidly falling behind our neighbors as we lacked the fundamentals to support startups.

So I did what any red-blooded entrepreneur would do, I created those fundamentals. Together with three other partners, whom admittedly I didn't know that well, we started the Stamford Innovation Center. Others had tried to get a similar idea to work, but our team of four finally struck the deal with the city and state to get it off the ground. We set up shop in the beautiful and historic old town hall of Stamford and quickly developed a co-working space, office space, and event space, which we filled with speakers and educational talks. It was a good launching pad for the entrepreneurial ecosystem in Connecticut.

Of course it didn't go smoothly and, ultimately, two of the partners dropped out. I hung in there with the remaining partner, who put in most of the effort, and we grew things to a reasonable level. As 2012 progressed, we hosted our first Stamford Startup Weekend and finally got some attention for the Connecticut entrepreneurial scene. With the beginnings of the ecosystem unveiled, I started to think again about launching a startup of my own and not just helping others with theirs.

CЗСЗСЗСЗСЗСЗ

With Sofia's third and final LTR at CHOP, my time freed up dramatically. Once Sofia fully recovered, I partnered with another Bill whom I'd met at the Stamford Innovation Center and together we founded MediaCrossing, a digital marketing and trading firm that brought together Wall Street (me) and Madison Avenue (him). We would bring algorithms and quantitative awesomeness to the Wild, Wild West of ad trading.

Bill and I started working out of the Innovation Center. It was great to use something I'd help build to launch my own company. We were both still part-time bootstrapping so I could be at home when I needed to even though Sofia's care didn't take as much time as it used to.

Bill and I were trying hard to find that first slug of money beyond our own capital that would make everything solidify. At this early stage, our company was an abstraction that we were willing into reality. Part of me was apprehensive because bringing in outside capital would be the full commitment point and drastically reduce my available time for the kids. But I needed to prove that I could do it. I needed it for me.

While we were pulling things together for MediaCrossing, my brother got married. His wedding was scheduled five weeks after Sofia's final LTR. That timing was tight. Even worse was the location—going

My brother Tim (left) and I.

into the thin oxygen of the Mile High City was not the best idea for someone who had just started to breathe through her mouth and nose. Denver was also three-quarters of the way across the country.

It was family, though, and you do what you have to.

As it turned out, the doctors weren't in consensus on whether or not Sofia could fly yet. We ultimately decided against it because we couldn't bring an emergency oxygen tank on board should Sofia really need one. And so we started a new tradition of Yang family road trips by driving from Connecticut to Colorado and back. We've since done many road trips throughout the world.

While I was on this first road trip, we secured commitment from a major investor for MediaCrossing; Sofia successfully breathed both in Denver and in Boulder; and we had a blast traveling throughout the country in our car, seeing America. It seemed as if things were all coming together for me to make this next jump in my professional life. I knew that, when I returned to Connecticut, I would take up the true mantle of founder-entrepreneur, working full-time for myself.

One important piece was missing though, health insurance. My family was still part of Tudor's plan through COBRA, but that wouldn't last forever. As founders, Bill and I agreed that we needed great health insurance. This brings me to the second lesson that I learned from my children (and Ray at Bridgewater): Take care of your people. Health insurance is a must. Great benefits attract great people and if you protect their families, they will work that much harder for you.

How, though, would we be able to affordably get great insurance for our company? The Affordable Care Act helped out by eliminating pre-existing conditions, but that didn't mean that insurers couldn't jack up the premiums because of our preemies. The answer we ultimately arrived at was joining a PEO (Professional Employer Organization)—allowing us to pool with many, many more people than were in our startup alone, which in turn allowed access to really good plans that were still expensive, but at least possible for a new company.

I say good plans and not great because they lacked things like 24-hour nursing. Our American health system just isn't equipped to handle that level of support, to the detriment of the families that need it. What that means is that families get stretched beyond what they can do with the limited nursing coverage they have and have to go into debt and in some cases bankruptcy. Or it means that babies have to go back to the hospital when they could otherwise be at home, running up costs and breaking apart families unnecessarily. This needs to change.

 CRCRCRCRCR

When I was first starting out as a manager, I believed that more is more. After all, I was at a Wall Street bank with thousands of people working for it.

When I moved to hedge funds, they all claimed to be lean and mean, but the reality was something different. People still brought their big-company mentality with them. They called it "leverage" instead of headcount, but the idea was the same—grow bigger and do more. Get someone to do your job then jump and take your boss's job. Every place I went to did the same thing: They grew and grew.

Post-kids, I thought that I had learned my lesson. I moved to smaller companies, including ones I started. Again the pressure to grow was everywhere. Venture capitalists want you to take more money and spend more money so you need more money from them and they get more of your company. After all, they earn their fees on the money they deploy, not what sits in the bank.

At MediaCrossing we ultimately took too much money and grew too fast; I finally learned that the goal of more wasn't the right goal, even for a startup. The right goal was growth per unit capital and

Supporting entrpreneurs while being one myself. Photo Credit: Sandro Art Photography

management effort: If you can earn a dollar with half the cost, then you are doing twice as well. Conversely, if it takes you three times as much management attention, you aren't doing that well at all. *You* are the least scalable resource and a common point of failure.

How did I come to this conclusion? This is exactly what it was like to manage Sofia's nurses.

Finding nurses was hard, and we would have issues where nurses couldn't make it on short notice. Your initial thought might be that more nurses would be better so that we would always have backup. But that isn't the case.

Having more nurses meant that individual nurses would get fewer hours. If they didn't get enough hours, they would take more hours elsewhere, which meant it was even less likely they would be available to fill a gap. Additionally, more nurses meant training new people and longer gaps between shifts of the same nurse, which meant Christine and I needed to spend more time to get them up to speed. It took more management attention to find and maintain a larger group of nurses for less incremental benefit.

When I make decisions for my companies now, I think about how much capital it will take as well as how much personal effort it will take. I also think about the worst-case scenario: Will it be overwhelming to me if things go wrong? This has resulted in slower but more measured—and I think sustainable—growth.

That lesson is something that founders need to internalize. It's the third lesson I learned from my preemies about entrepreneurship.

Before Sofia and Daniel were born, would I have started any company on my own? Definitely not. I was too afraid of failure. My career had bumps, but pretty much went in one direction, up. I thought that I took risks, but they were always super-calculated and within the framework of the financial institution I worked at, so they weren't really risks at all.

Compare that to the many, many decisions that had to be made regarding Sofia's care and the powerlessness of knowing that, no matter what you did, something would likely go wrong. All that I could do was prepare, try my best, and be ready to make quick decisions when crisis hit.

If it hadn't have been for my premature triplets, there is no way I would have taken the leap to put myself and millions of dollars at risk for a dream of launching a startup. Going through our tragedy put everything in perspective. Fighting for Sofia and Daniel helped me understand what I really valued and taught me important lessons. Without our preemies, I would've continued to be highly paid but under-satisfied.

.

CHAPTER 10

ACCEPTING NEW DREAMS

*"The big, crazy challenge of keeping Sofia alive
these past four years has been accomplished...
The adventure will continue on."*
—*The Yang Triplets Blog, September 3, 2012*

It isn't an exaggeration to say that I like doing everything fast. I pride myself on my ability to understand things rapidly and quickly climb up any learning curve. I was one of those precocious kids who would take things apart to understand how they worked. If I was really lucky, I'd be able to put it back together again—when I was three, my dad's very expensive camera was not so lucky.

As I got older, my parents spared no expense buying me anything that had educational value. I got my first computer in second grade, when having one in your house was still a relatively new and expensive thing. My parents didn't get me an actual Apple II. Instead, they got me a Taiwanese knock-off that *mostly* worked. However, that turned out to be a good thing. My uncle had put it together for me, and since he was in far off Washington, D.C., and the "manual" was a few booklets of unintelligible Chinese, I had to learn to fix things myself when they went wrong.

Like pretty much every parent I know, I thought that having a child, a mini-me, would be cool. I could correct all of the countless mistakes my parents made with me, be a tough but "Cool Dad," and, importantly, get a second chance to redo my own tough moments growing up. All the while I would be the perfectly supportive and understanding dad, helping my children reach their full potential.

And there was no doubt I would make sure my children learned how to catch a ball, swing a bat, throw a football, skate, ski, and not have my challenges with hand-eye coordination. They would master all of this at a young age.

All of that went out the window when our preemies were born. For my kids, survival was a miracle in and of itself. In those first years before Sofia got off her trach, I didn't have the time to think about anything more than keeping her alive. As things got easier for Sofia, I started to think again about what their lives and my life would be like.

I didn't like where those thoughts took me.

My daughter was out of the woods in terms of emergent health problems, but she was far, far behind. Other kids had been eating solid food for years, including Daniel, but Sofia couldn't even swallow, and she was just figuring out how to use her voice.

We also discovered while she was still in Birth to Three that her balance was off. The root cause was unknown, but likely it was due to lack of oxygen during her seizures in the NICU that affected her brain. Hemiplegia was not something that resolved itself and possibly was a very mild form of cerebral palsy.

This meant that Sofia learned to walk with the help of a therapist, and even to this day, she cannot run properly. She gets treatments to balance out the tightness in her leg muscles so that she can walk more easily. She has to be careful going up and down the stairs. She tires quickly and, while her stamina continues to improve, it isn't quite what a typical child has.

When—how—could I teach her to skate or kick a ball?

I was face-to-face with the reality that my daughter would be disabled for the rest of her life. I know that I should be thankful that her disabilities are minor. There are many, many other kids with far more severe disabilities and conditions. But she is so, so close to typical that it hurts me, as it would any parent. Especially as I know other kids won't give her a break about it. I was picked on as the only Chinese kid in the school and I expect the same will eventually happen to her because of her disabilities. Kids intentionally and unintentionally can be horrible to each other.

On top of that, even the things that I was able to do early on and love, like singing, she would be unable to do. She was still eating ground up food at five years old; no amount of practice would get her to Carnegie Hall's stage.

I took these realizations hard, but not in an obvious way. In fact, other than by reading this, I would bet that my wife and my friends have little idea just how crushing it was for me. I had to readjust my dreams for my child and I felt selfish, frustrated, and sad that I wouldn't be having those afternoon catches in the yard or singing with Sofia. And what about the more distant future? I couldn't let myself go there.

Christine, too, had similar thoughts. During the preschool program, Christine became friends with some of the moms she met there and together they learned how to mourn their vision of a child that was "normal." It was Christine's opportunity to just be a mom—to talk about her kids and swap stories.

Still though, Sofia was able to get off her trach, so part of me hoped that she would improve and develop ways to get around and get past her physical disabilities and that medical technology would find a way to help her.

CRCRCRCRCR

We were definitely counting on modern science to help with her voice. As it turned out, her three LTRs (and possibly her initial respiratory issues) had left her vocal chords severely damaged. Her voice post-trach was abnormal, soft and raspy—and not in a future Lauren-Bacall-kind-of-way (look her up if you don't know who she is). After a few doctor visits, we discovered that it would likely be that way permanently.

She was suffering from a triple-threat of vocal chord issues. One chord was higher than the other, leaving an air gap; part of one did not open and close properly—perhaps due to nerve damage; and her airway was disturbed with scarring and other damage.

As it turned out, CHOP had a leading expert in the field, Dr. Zur, who was in the same ENT practice as Dr. Jacobs and focused exclusively on the voice. She had done pioneering work in improving the vocal quality of children through surgical intervention. We went to see her a few times and she examined Sofia at length with a scope while under anesthesia.

The conclusion was that at her age (four), there were essentially zero permanent treatments that could be done. In some adults, nerves have been transplanted to improve chord motility, but not in children—and not in multiple-LTR patients.

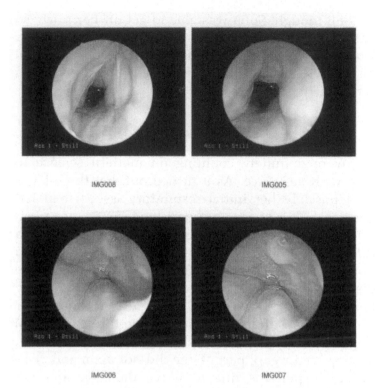

IMG008   IMG005

IMG006   IMG007

Sofia's reconstructed airway showing her misaligned vocal chords in the top-left image.

The one thing that Dr. Zur considered trying was an injection of gel into her vocal chords that would "plump" them up in an attempt to give her better volume and tone control by reducing the air gap between them.

Why not give it a shot? Compared to the LTRs, this surgery was trivial, and we were old hands at putting Sofia under anesthesia. We tried the surgery and waited to see if there were any positive effects. Unfortunately, because Sofia was very small for her age, Dr. Zur couldn't get much gel into her vocal chords and the impact turned out to be very small. We tried a few more times over the next two years as Sofia grew larger, but ultimately gave up on the treatment as it didn't appear to do anything to improve the quality of her voice.

More drastic measures might be possible as she becomes an adult and reaches her full growth. The risks will likely still be extremely high, possibly fatal, so it will be her decision.

03030303030

By the time their fifth birthday approached, Sofia improved in her ability to eat, even if that still meant ground-up paste. Both she and Daniel remained on the very bottom of the growth charts but steady gains were regularly made.

Their nurses and most of their health issues were now either behind them or well on the track to resolution. The way I tell it, the kids still had medical issues, but none of them were urgent or critical; we didn't have to worry every day about Sofia dying on us.

We still saw way too many doctors, but even that was tailing off. The kids were steadily growing despite a few scares about nutrition, and growth fixes a lot of problems.

After the third LTR, my mother and Jane moved out and we were finally a "typical" American family of four. We still had help with meals, cleaning, and watching the kids, we just stopped having a live-in. Thus our family returned to some sense of normalcy just as I truly became a full-time entrepreneur in the fall of 2012 with the launch of MediaCrossing.

My mother returned to Baltimore and continued to operate the family-owned chemical company in China, which is one of the companies I am a founding investor of. Jane, who by then was well on her way to mastering English and overall improving her education, moved on to another family. Last I heard, she had moved to California where she is a successful Chinese doula/midwife serving wealthy Chinese-American families.

Their leaving meant no more exposure to Mandarin for Sofia and Daniel, the language they had regularly heard from Grandma and Jane the first four years of their lives. We never worried about confusing them with dual languages. They were pretty good at asking for things in Chinese, but have lost it all since. I hope

Daniel and Sofia with their Grandma.

that because they heard the sounds and tones of Chinese in their formative years, it will provide a good underpinning for them if they choose to study Mandarin again in the future. (And I hope they do.)

ଔଔଔଔଔ

So much of this story focuses on Sofia because her problems were life or death, but Daniel had his own non-life-threatening issues over the years, too. It was easy to overlook what was going on: His problems were important, but they weren't as urgent.

For Daniel, his issues were in his head—by his third birthday he was diagnosed with autism.

We knew that due to prematurity he would be developmentally delayed, and that came to pass. He crawled a little later than other babies, stood a little later than other toddlers, and was always a little small. It's a little unnerving to have parents touting on Facebook that their kids are 90th or higher percentile when Daniel didn't even make the chart.

Daniel showed absolutely no developmental delays in reading, and, in fact, he started reading extremely early. Christine disputes this, but I know that he was reading aloud before his second birthday. He read all of his baby books to us and more—and it wasn't just that he had memorized them from listening to us read them to him.

It turns out that this super-encouraging development, known as hyperlexia and defined as a precocious and self-developing ability to read, was the first sign of autism. This diagnosis became clearer still when his level of interaction was obviously below that of other children as the years went by: Daniel didn't initiate play and didn't talk spontaneously.

Speech therapy was one of the things the Birth to Three program worked on. Sofia would babble at just about anything (even with her trach) and was a color-commentary reporter about her day-to-day life. Daniel

Daniel watching his favorite show, Jeopardy!

was always quiet and didn't respond to you unless you specifically got his attention.

Autism was first picked up by Birth to Three and confirmed after further testing. This was right before our kids were handed off to the New Canaan preschool. He was "on the spectrum" with mild affect, mostly social affect. Other than that, Daniel didn't act out or have behavioral issues, but he did perseverate (repeating nonsense sentences like in the film "Rain Man") and as he grew older, he did a significant amount of self-stimulation, or "stimming," usually via playing with a pointy object by waving it in the air. He was especially fond of repeating random fragments of the pharmaceutical commercials, which aired during "Jeopardy!" It started off as cute but quickly had us worried.

His diagnosis was relatively mild and his prognosis was a pretty good one, but as with most things related to autism, it was far too early to tell.

I'm certainly not qualified to speak for all Asians, but from personal experience, the behaviors that signal mild autism aren't necessarily worrying for many Asians, in fact, they are selected for. Having a child that focuses obsessively on words and numbers but doesn't waste time chit-chatting? What an obedient son! Having a child that's always quiet and behaves nicely? Sounds perfect!

What this means is that to this day, my mother, an otherwise brilliant woman—a scientist—doesn't really get that autism isn't something that can be worked past or that Daniel isn't "just shy."

I was "just shy" as a kid myself.

My parents bought a house in the best school district they could afford, all to give my brother and me the best educational opportunities. They didn't count on how racist and just plain terrible kids could be to each other. Couple that with my overachieving, teacher's pet attitude towards school (once again from my parents; my mom was one of the original "Tiger Moms"), and I was a target with a capital T. I was bullied, picked on, and humiliated with racial slurs at least weekly. Bear in mind, this was the post-Vietnam era when saying "gook" and "chink," usually accompanied by the obligatory eye-pulling, was A-OK, even by adults. As it turned out, the only full-Asians other than me at my school were actual Vietnamese refugees that had been brought back from the war. They didn't deserve this kind of treatment and neither did I.

My parents, mostly my mom, would tell me that bullying and racism didn't matter and that I would ultimately have the last laugh because I would succeed in life and they would be miserable failures. That didn't really help me when I was living it.

In elementary school until about fifth grade I had few friends and was an introverted little kid. But was I "just shy," or did I too have mild autism?

In retrospect, I think that I did have several symptoms of autism—for example ADD (Attention Deficit Disorder)—and that I still do. If tested, these could've landed me on the spectrum. But back in the late 1970s, autism wasn't a real thing to most parents and definitely not to my Asian parents.

I know it wasn't real to my parents because I'm pretty sure my father is a highly functioning autistic, with what they used to call Aspergers Syndrome, even though he has never sought diagnoses nor been diagnosed as such.

Now that I know what to look for, I can see that he has many of the behaviors and social issues of autistic people. This understanding came too late for my father and me ever to be close, but it does shed some light on exactly what this diagnosis could mean for his grandson, both positive and negative.

When Daniel was initially diagnosed, I was in some denial about it; Christine, however, saw it as no surprise, having picked up on the strong indications for it. Part of me was focused on the life-threatening problems Sofia was dealing with. Part of me also agreed with my mother and hoped he'd grow out of it. Now I can label it for what it was: wishful thinking.

I covered my denial by having Daniel go through more observations and more tests under the guise of gathering more data. Further testing was totally legitimate and something that the school district wanted to do and paid for, but it was a delaying action nonetheless.

My denial was all about trying to avoid labeling him.

I knew how hard it was to be labeled as different based upon my skin color and the slant of my eyes. My son would have those labels just like I did and, on top of that, would also be a "spectrum kid"—potentially much worse. I thought that the autism label would doom him to be even more lonely than I was as a child. I wanted to do everything I could to avoid it. I mean seriously, hadn't our kids been through enough already?

Then around the time when Sofia was preparing for her third and final reconstruction something flipped in my mind. The power of the label was certainly real, but I realized that while a label could hurt him, it could also help him. Getting Daniel his proper diagnosis would unlock a universe of care and, while there might never be a "cure," the mild nature of his diagnosis meant that he could develop coping skills and possibly still live a "typical" life.

I also learned that a label was, in fact, something that other parents wanted for their children. Not necessarily full-blown autism, but something milder such as ADD or ADHD would give their child special accommodations in school. They could then leverage that label into getting additional test time, bonus credit on tests, the ability to redo assignments, or have easier homework; they used the label to receive special allowances for doing the same work. Some parents— and I've met them—actually believe that getting little junior labeled as ADD means an easier path for him to get into Harvard. It's not uncommon around where I live for parents to hold back their kids a year before starting school so that they are larger for sports teams and thus gain an advantage over other kids. Is this really any different?

Our school district was alert to these types of games and tried very hard to prevent them. The plus side of this meant that the school was ready, willing, and able to help kids who actually had issues like Daniel and Sofia. They wanted to give these kids all of the care they needed and then some.

I'm a pretty adversarial person. I grew up with a "me vs. them" mindset that I attribute to being a lone minority and the hazing I received because of it. My parents raised me to believe that I needed to constantly look out for myself and fight for myself.

I had heard horror stories about special education in neighboring Darien, which is just as wealthy and white as New Canaan. In that district, they had had amazing Special Ed programs until a new superintendent came to town. He cut all of it to the bone, far beyond what was legal and redirected the money to other things—like extra uniforms for the sports teams. The administration actively pushed back against the parents they had previously supported and denied their children the services they needed. As a result, Special Ed in Darien was a nightmare that ended in state intervention, mass resignations, and lawsuits galore.

Nearby Greenwich was also infamous for resisting special accommodations for students. To be fair they have a great Special Ed program, but they have a cookie-cutter approach to it, are take-it-or-leave-it with families, and bring their lawyers to parent meetings.

Therefore, after Daniel got his diagnosis, I was ready to fight our school district to get him everything he needed. I didn't think anybody would deny Sofia the care and accommodations she needed for her physical issues, but Daniel was a much milder case, and I figured the bean counters would try to even up the Yang family accounts or something. I didn't lawyer up, but I did everything just short, speaking to numerous professionals about the approach to take and developing many levels of negotiating plans. Negotiating, after all, is pretty much what I do for a living.

I shouldn't have bothered. From the first meeting the room was filled full of therapists, counselors, teachers, and administrators that would be taking care

Sofia and Daniel, April 2011.

of my children. They already knew Sofia and Daniel and really cared about them. We have never had to fight for anything we needed for Daniel and Sofia. In fact, our experience has been exactly the opposite. Our school suggests programs and support to give our kids, even when it obviously costs them serious time and money to do so—and even when that is after school or during the summer.

Special needs parents, please don't take my story as a guidebook for how to do it. You are better off being paranoid and being over-prepared. Many similar situations are adversarial; the huge dollars and all the lawyers involved bias it that way.

෨෩෨෩෨෩෨෩෨෩

Since the label of "autism" could help Daniel get services to help him live in a "typical" world and to lead a "typical" life, I learned to accept it. But I still struggled because there was nothing concrete to blame for his situation

Just as our triplets were born, the anti-vax movement was growing full-steam. Nevertheless, we wanted our surviving children vaccinated. Christine and I are children of educators and scientists and we don't subscribe to paranoia.

The standard vaccination schedule from the Centers for Disease Control specifies that newborns should receive a Hepatitis B vaccine upon birth, then another a month later, and then at two months a whole slew of other vaccines.

Under normal circumstances, Christine and I would not have hesitated to vaccinate on schedule. However, when faced with vaccinating our super-preemies, we had to think carefully.

Typically, doctors like to vaccinate preemies as soon as possible. The protocol for babies under 2000 grams (approximately 4.4 pounds) is to wait until one month of age and then get them back on the regular schedule for the obvious reason that any of the diseases being vaccinated for would be instantly fatal given the babies' highly critical state. That was the pro side. But I saw a con side, too—at least initially. I questioned whether vaccination made sense given their micro-size, immature immune systems, and possible side effects, specifically around mercury and thimerosal.

Our doctors did not hesitate in their response: They explained that preemies have operating immune systems and that the benefits far outweighed the risks Also, their vaccines didn't use thimerosal and hadn't for decades.

There hadn't been many studies, but I did find one paper about preemie vaccination that supported their claims. After consultation with Dr. Bob, who emphatically concurred and had never seen a negative reaction to vaccination other than egg allergies, we had Sofia and Daniel vaccinated.

Does Daniel have autism because of vaccination? Absolutely, positively not.

How am I so sure? I'm a rational human being who has done the research and believes in science over hype. The doctors who had gotten Sofia and Daniel so far believed vaccination was appropriate, and, more importantly, so did Dr. Bob, a doctor who had my complete trust and who had reviewed the cases of tens of thousands of preemies in his distinguished career. That was enough for me.

Autism *is* scary and not something anyone wants to live with. I get why parents need something to blame.

Choosing to delay vaccination (or not) lets you feel like you're actively in control of your child's health. But not vaccinating actively causes harm to your child and others who rely on shared immunity.

ॐॐॐॐॐ

As relieved as I was that things were working out in terms of support, they weren't fully working out enough for me. I wanted my son to do everything that I hadn't/didn't/couldn't do and to make up for mistakes that I myself had made. I know I'm not the lone father to want such.

If you meet me now, you'd consider me a strong personality, but I wasn't always this way and especially not in grade school. I profoundly regret that.

Now my son was going to walk down that same path. This wasn't just selfish. I know first-hand how lonely it was for me. It was and it is still hard for me to think that he will always be "different" and won't be the "cool kid" that I never was. Even worse, it is hard for me to think that he might not ever have deep friendships. I made common cause with other nerds and loners and ultimately made friends starting in fourth grade. I know I'm dramatizing a bit, but it is hard for me, as Daniel doesn't have the same level of friendships that I had at his age, now 12. I've already had to ratchet down my dreams of my children being little prodigies and sports stars, now my expectations were being reset yet again further downward.

I didn't panic when we started noticing similar behaviors in Sofia. It was harder for Christine this time around since unlike with Daniel, Sofia had always been so verbal. She didn't perseverate but she did stim and have sensory issues. Neither of my kids does well with loud noises, which can cause them to cover their ears and run out of a room. Sofia especially is sensitive to emotional content and can start crying when people

Sofia is happy to be turning four.

applaud too loudly or just sing "Happy Birthday." We had her tested, too, and, yes, she is on the spectrum but not with the same social affect as Daniel. She clearly has sensory issues but also mild behavioral issues and rigidity, meaning that she has set ways of behavior and it could be difficult for her to be flexible about things like her schedule—way beyond other kids.

Again I asked: What more could life throw at us? We had cleared the hurdles for life-threatening medical issues that most parents never ever have to go through and couldn't even imagine. Now we were being hit with a double-dose of autism, which in Sofia's case is coupled with physical weakness and voice issues that will persist her entire life. My children are both special needs kids.

I had to wonder, would my kids be able to live independent, fulfilled, and happy lives? A new set of high and long hurdles were coming into view and as I write this, we are just figuring out how we will jump over them.

When we told my mom, she didn't truly understand what this meant, perhaps because she never really identified it in my father. As educators, Christine's parents knew much more what we were about to be getting into. All of them were as supportive as we could want them to be, despite having to deal with their own lives.

Finding out about Sofia did rule out our having more children. The strongest predictor of whether or not you will have a premature child is having had one in the past. Christine thought she wanted more children, but I knew that I would not be able to go through what we'd been through already again. It is one thing to go through tragedy not knowing what to expect. It is quite another to do it again knowing how bad it could be for you and for your child. In addition, this time around, Sofia and Daniel would be impacted by any new preemies, and they needed our attention to work through their special needs. It wouldn't be fair to them to spread our attention and resources even thinner.

While writing my story, it was presented to me that the companies I found and help as an entrepreneur are my additional "children." Perhaps in a way they are. I can certainly partly define myself by their successes and failures.

Yet if Sofia's life-threatening experience has taught me anything, it is hope. Hope in science and medicine and hope in love. I have hope that we will advance our children through their difficulties and get all of us out the other side. I have hope that Daniel will make friendships on his own terms and that the world recognizes the value of autistic people everywhere.

Epilogue

Tiny Miracles

It has taken years for me to write this much. I first started playing with writing this book two years ago and had a few false starts. I only really made progress on it when I discovered that my most productive writing time is when I'm at an airport or on a plane, especially if the wifi isn't reliable, which is often the case.

Since it has been so long, it is easy for me to forget why I started down this journey in the first place.

Why did I choose to write this book? A need for catharsis.

I've never properly mourned Raymond and I've never before admitted to myself much of what I've written in these pages. By sorting out events in my own mind and then committing them to paper, I've started the process of healing myself by laying out my origin story as a father.

These pages are my way of understanding myself and looking at how I've succeeded and failed—from my own perspective and that of others.

They are also my way of connecting with other parents and fathers especially. You won't find many books for dads (let alone written by dads) going through something like what I've been through. I never found any books that could've have shown me I wasn't alone when I was in need.

Do fathers talk about loss with each other? We should. I only discovered that people I'd known for years had lost children after I told them of my family's struggle.

Not only is this book about my becoming a father, but it's also about my becoming an entrepreneur. The two will forever be linked for me. With children, my life is much more meaningful and interesting than it was before—both at work and at home. This is not where I thought I would be at 45, but I'm glad life gave me a shove off of the path I was walking. I had to do my own growing up in order to find my way.

So if you are a father or soon-to-be father, this book is your permission slip to tell your story and know that you are not alone. We *need* your story. Please share your experiences—both highs and lows—with other fathers. You will never know how much it means to a fellow father to hear about your struggles, your victories, your life, and your children.

What kept me going when the writing bogged down was the fact that my family's story is not over. I know that things happen for a reason. I've felt that way ever since I was young. Maybe that's my own disordered mind grasping at straws and needing an explanation to keep going, but it works for me.

Do I regret making the decision we made to keep all three of our children? No. I wish that I had Raymond in my life, but not at the price of Sofia.

Did the decision to keep all three cause my children's disabilities? That's a bit harder for me to say. I know that rationally our decision to go forward with all three did not cause their special needs, but still I feel responsible. Loving them despite their challenges, especially the resetting of my expectations for them— for us—is in part my penance for my hubris that we could have three typical children without any difficulties.

C3C3C3C3C3

It has been 12 years since our triplets were born. Our survivors, Sofia and Daniel just started sixth grade in Saxe Middle School in New Canaan. They continue to each have an army of supporters both in and out of school that are doing everything they can for them with the ultimate goal of turning them into fully functional adults.

Sometimes, however, that feels very far away. I've had fuller conversations with kindergartners than I've had with Daniel. Sofia can be articulate when she chooses to be, but that's rare. She lives in the moment and gets stuck on one topic like children many years younger than she do. Both kids are struggling to make connections now that everything is on Zoom.

Early readers have asked me if the strangers in the introduction refer to my own children. That wasn't my original intent, but it does hold a grain of truth. I long for the day when we can all have dinner table conversations together. It crushes me to think that might never happen and it is hard for me as a father to not know how I can help make that happen.

Sofia is exhibiting more behavioral problems as (gasp!) she enters puberty, but her physical issues continue to get better as she grows larger and gets stronger. Her voice is still raspy and difficult to understand, but the strong force of her personality means that she has friends and that she always gets per point across. She thinks lots of things are funny, even when they are not, and occasionally her sensory issues keep her from interacting typically with others. Her empathy is especially strong and she likes to be highly organized. Sofia loves arts and crafts, especially watching videos on YouTube and then cutting apart Daniel's books! Sofia has my temper and she can't eat a meal without making a mess on her clothes. She is clearly my daughter.

The kids on their first day of middle school August, 2019

Daniel is sweet, loving, and super kind—like his mother. Other kids respond well to that and so far he hasn't been picked on or bullied. His autism makes it hard for him socially. He loves video games and has an infallible sense of direction. Even when we are driving in other countries, he intuitively knows the way back to our home away from home. He is usually quiet and alone, and I worry that he doesn't have any close friends. But I do see signs that therapy and coping skills are starting to work. He especially comes out of his shell for music and swimming.

Both kids continue to do well academically, although not on standardized tests—exactly unlike their father but exactly like their mother. As the years go on, it will become more and more difficult for them to keep up. We hope that they reach a level of accommodation with their special needs that enables them to learn together with their typical peers.

The other day, Christine's parents along with her sister and her family paid us a visit. Despite being younger, both of Sofia and Daniel's cousins are vastly more articulate and mature, a living reminder of Sofia and Daniel's developmental delays.

And yet, that hasn't changed at all how their grandparents have interacted with them. When I see them playing together it doesn't matter that they are developmentally delayed; love is unconditional.

Christine has returned to work part-time. She still shoulders most of the responsibility for the children and I thank her for it. Even though there is more for us to deal with as parents than for those with average kids, now that they are in school there is a lot more time for my wife to be herself again. She has spent a lot of time working with Tiny Miracles, a local non-profit that exists to help the families of those with preemies, most recently as their vice president. As we know first-hand, those families need all the support they can get. You can find out more at *www.ttmf.org*.

And me? I've started 13 companies and counting, including non-profit companies, for-profit companies, and of course, inadvertently not-profitable companies—also known as failures. I work on several now at the same time and fully indulge my adult ADD.

Currently, my primary effort is running 4-CT, a new non-profit that a friend, Don Kendall, and I created to drive COVID-19 relief statewide. It's a mostly volunteer effort (of more than 25 people). We pass along 100 percent of what we take in to front-line non-profits that are helping those disproportionately affected by this crisis in Connecticut. Since mid-March we've made over $20 million in impact. We've also created the first statewide direct aid program, the 4-CT Card. You can find out more at 4-ct.org.

ೞೞೞೞೞ

Parenting is never easy and our journey has been and will continue to be especially difficult. Our lives are clearly different from other families that don't have two special needs kids, but I think our day-to-day struggles are much like any other family would experience: We work on making our kids more independent, stopping them from fighting with each other, trying to teach them right from wrong, and so on. We go out and do the same family things that other families do, or rather did, in that near-mythical pre-COVID world. While we do have other friends with special needs kids, perhaps the biggest difference between my family and a "typical" family is that we shoulder a lot of the burden ourselves because there are fewer peer parents we can interact with.

There are four key points I would advise any parent going through a similar situation to keep in mind:

1. You are your child's best advocate, the only one who knows holistically what your child needs. Do not let your concerns be

discounted or your child's needs waved away.

2. Part of knowing how to best advocate for your child is to be well informed. Ask questions, read and learn on your own. It's a crash course in a topic you never wanted to study but now very much need to.

3. Don't assume healthcare providers have the whole picture. They are benefited by you having the details at your fingertips. Prepare a one-pager/cheat sheet. It may save you valuable time.

4. Find a way to step away from it all—at least for a little while—every now and then. Respite matters. This is an ultra-marathon and not a sprint. Your child needs you at your best, or as close to it as you can get.

If there's any *one* thing a father (or mother) going through a similar situation should take away from my story, it's that you're not alone. Others can help—and you may find this help in unexpected places. Find your Dr. Bob—your confessor, your support, your confidant, your friend. Talk about it.

When I tell someone our story, I'm often hit with how incredulous they are that we got through it. Truth is, we don't really know ourselves how we managed it. You play the hand you are dealt and try not to look over your shoulder at other people's cards. I have hope that our journey has a purpose: One day Daniel and Sofia will look back and read these pages as happy, fulfilled adults

.

ABOUT THE AUTHOR

The son of Chinese immigrants, Ted Yang was born in Suffern, NY. He and his wife Christine have a surviving son with Autism and a daughter with physical disabilities, both aged 12.

Ted is a serial entrepreneur who has founded 13 startups and non-profits. These include: Cantata Media/Daily Voice, Highclere Castle Spirits, MediaCrossing, the Stamford Innovation Center, and 4-CT.

Prior to that, Ted was an executive at the world's most successful hedge funds, including Bridgewater and Citadel. He has sat on several notable boards including the Wiki Education Foundation and the Meadville-Lombard Theological School.

Ted finished his Masters of Engineering at MIT at 21, has been featured in the *Wall Street Journal,* NPR and Fox Business News, and has spoken at the MIT, Wharton, Babson, NYU, and Columbia Business Schools.

Made in the USA
Middletown, DE
16 November 2020

24227800R00116